EXPLORERS
AND
EXPLORATION

HAKLUYT, RICHARD – LA VÉRENDRYE, PIERRE GAULTIER DE

Marshall Cavendish
New York • London • Singapore

Marshall Cavendish
99 White Plains Road
Tarrytown, New York 10591-9001

www.marshallcavendish.com

Consultants: Ralph Ehrenberg, former chief, Geography
and Map Division, Library of Congress, Washington, DC;
Conrad Heidenreich, former historical geography
professor, York University, Toronto; Shane Winser,
information officer, Royal Geographical Society, London

Contributing authors: Dale Anderson, Kay Barnham,
Peter Chrisp, Richard Dargie, Paul Dowswell, Elizabeth
Gogerly, Steven Maddocks, John Malam, Stewart Ross,
Shane Winser

MARSHALL CAVENDISH
Editor: Thomas McCarthy
Editorial Director: Paul Bernabeo
Production Manager: Michael Esposito

WHITE-THOMSON PUBLISHING
Editors: Alex Woolf and Steven Maddocks
Design: Derek Lee and Ross George
Cartographer: Peter Bull Design
Picture Research: Glass Onion Pictures
Indexer: Fiona Barr

ISBN 0-7614-7535-4 (set)
ISBN 0-7614-7540-0 (vol. 5)

Printed in China

08 07 06 05 04 5 4 3 2 1

color key	time period
▬▬▬	to 500
▬▬▬	500–1400
▬▬▬	1400–1850
▬▬▬	1850–1945
▬▬▬	1945–2000
▬▬▬	general articles

Library of Congress Cataloging-in-Publication Data
Explorers and exploration.
    p. cm.
  Includes bibliographical references (p.   ) and index.
  ISBN 0-7614-7535-4 (set : alk. paper) -- ISBN 0-7614-
7536-2 (v. 1) -- ISBN 0-7614-7537-0 (v. 2) -- ISBN 0-7614-
7538-9 (v. 3) -- ISBN 0-7614-7539-7 (v. 4) -- ISBN 0-7614-
7540-0 (v. 5) -- ISBN 0-7614-7541-9 (v. 6) -- ISBN 0-7614-
7542-7 (v. 7) -- ISBN 0-7614-7543-5 (v. 8) -- ISBN 0-7614-
7544-3 (v. 9) -- ISBN 0-7614-7545-1 (v. 10) -- ISBN 0-
7614-7546-X (v. 11)
  1. Explorers--Encyclopedias. 2. Discoveries in
geography--Encyclopedias. I. Marshall Cavendish
Corporation. II. Title.
  G80.E95 2005
  910'.92'2--dc22

                          2004048292

CONTENTS

HAKLUYT, RICHARD

THE ENGLISH SCHOLAR AND WRITER Richard Hakluyt (c. 1552–1616) spent a lifetime collecting and publishing accounts of voyages of exploration. A driving force behind the English voyages of the period, he played an important role in the early colonization of North America and in the search for both the Northeast and the Northwest Passages.

Below **This painting of Hakluyt, one of the few in existence, is carried aboard the cruise liner RMS** *Queen Mary*, **now moored permanently at Long Beach, California.**

Richard Hakluyt was born in London and educated at Westminster School, where he learned Greek and Latin, and Oxford University, where he studied French, Italian, Spanish, and Portuguese. He also developed a passion for geography and gave lectures on the subject. He was among the first to introduce the use of globes in schools and is considered Oxford University's first professor of modern geography. Hakluyt later took holy orders, but although he would earn a living from the church throughout his life, his real interest always lay in stories of exploration. In 1582 he published his first book, an account of voyages to North America, including those of John and Sebastian Cabot.

In 1583 Hakluyt was appointed chaplain to the English ambassador in France, Sir Edward Stafford. In Paris, Hakluyt discovered Giovanni da Verrazzano's unpublished account of his 1524 voyage to the Americas. In 1586 Hakluyt published a French edition of the work, and the next year he translated it into English.

c. 1552
Richard Hakluyt is born in London.

1580
Becomes Oxford's first professor of modern geography.

1582
Publishes *Divers Voyages Touching the Discovery of America*.

1583–1588
Serves as chaplain to the English ambassador in Paris.

1584
Writes *A Discourse on the Western Planting*.

1585
Walter Raleigh founds first English colony in North America and names it Virginia.

1587
A second North American colony is established on Roanoke Island, off the coast of Virginia .

1589
Hakluyt publishes first version of *Principal Navigations*.

1590
Becomes rector of Wetheringsett, Suffolk. Advises a company searching for the Northeast Passage.

1612
Helps found the Northwest Passage Company.

1616
Dies and is buried in Westminster Abbey.

1846
The Hakluyt Society is founded to preserve Richard Hakluyt's works and to publish other narratives of exploration.

Hakluyt made it his business to know all the prominent figures in English exploration, including the nobles and merchants who financed voyages and the sea captains who led them. Because of the reputation he gained for being well informed, Hakluyt was frequently employed as an adviser in the planning of expeditions. In 1590, for example, he advised a merchant company that was sending ships on a voyage to find the Northeast Passage. In the 1600s two English explorers, Henry Hudson and William Baffin, named a headland and an island, respectively, after Hakluyt in recognition of the assistance he had given them.

RALEIGH'S PLAN FOR A COLONY

One of Hakluyt's closest friends was Sir Walter Raleigh, the explorer, nobleman, and confidant of Queen Elizabeth I. Raleigh's dream was to found an English settlement in North America. In 1584 Hakluyt wrote, on Raleigh's behalf, *A Discourse on the Western Planting*. Its purpose was to persuade the queen to back Raleigh's scheme for the colonization of North America.

As a young boy Hakluyt first became interested in geography after seeing a world map belonging to his cousin and guardian, the lawyer Richard Hakluyt. He later wrote,

He seeing me somewhat curious . . . began to instruct my ignorance . . . he pointed with his wand to all the known seas, gulfs, bays, straits, capes, rivers, empires, kingdoms, dukedoms, and territories of each part, with declaration also of their commodities and particular wants, which by the benefit of traffic . . . are plentifully supplied.

Richard Hakluyt, *The Principal Navigations, Voyages and Discoveries of the English Nation*

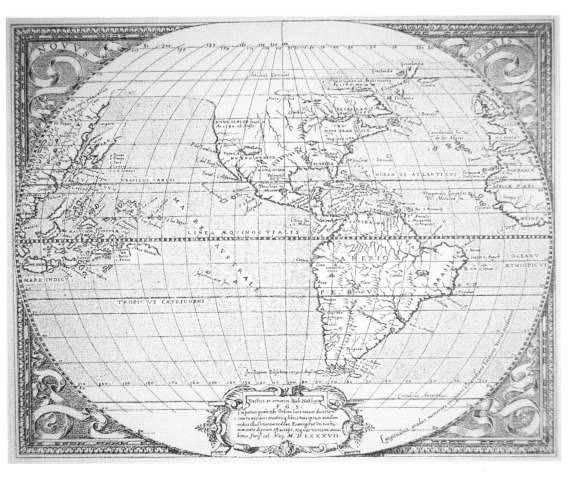

Left **Hakluyt's 1587 map of the New World reflects almost one hundred years of Spanish and Portuguese presence in the Americas, and although parts of the New World are drawn with remarkable accuracy, there is much, especially in North America, that is speculative or unknown.**

Hakluyt listed several objectives of English settlement in America: to spread the Protestant religion; to create new English trade; to supply England's needs from her own lands rather than from foreign countries; to provide work for unemployed men; to provide bases to attack the Spanish colonies in the Americas; to expand the Royal Navy; and to discover the Northwest Passage.

Queen Elizabeth gave Raleigh royal approval for his plan. In 1585 Raleigh sent four ships to America, where an English colony was founded; it was named Virginia, in honor of Elizabeth, the Virgin Queen. However, conflict with American Indians made this first settlement unsuccessful. In 1586 Sir Francis Drake rescued the starving colonists and took them home.

Neither Hakluyt nor Raleigh gave up after their first failure. Hakluyt helped Raleigh organize a second expedition, which in 1587 established a colony of 117 settlers on Roanoke Island, off the coast of Virginia. Three years later a relief voyage found the colony completely deserted. To this day it is not known what happened to the settlers.

PRINCIPAL NAVIGATIONS

Hakluyt's most important work was *The Principal Navigations, Voyages and Discoveries*

of the English Nation, published as a single volume in 1589. Ten years later, from 1598 to 1600, Hakluyt published an expanded version in three volumes that contained a million and a half words.

Hakluyt spent the rest of his life collecting accounts for an even larger edition of *Principal Navigations*. Although he died in 1616 before he could complete the work, his papers were acquired by Samuel Purchas, a fellow scholar. Purchas used Hakluyt's materials in his 1625 publication, *Purchas, His Pilgrims*, which is four million words long.

Hakluyt's *Principal Navigations* is a collection of accounts of English voyages, many of them recorded by eyewitnesses. Although it is full of gripping stories of adventure and heroism that are read for pure entertainment, Hakluyt's main motive was to write a practical book that would be useful to merchant companies and explorers. The work was taken to sea by English captains and often helped them in difficulty. In 1607, for example, an English fleet needed to find a safe place to anchor off the coast of Sierra Leone in Africa. The captain was able to find his anchorage thanks to the description of the coast in "the Book," as English sailors called *Principal Navigations*.

In 1592 the *Desire* returned across the Atlantic to England after a terrible winter near the southern tip of South America. *Principal Navigations* includes this harrowing account, written by John Jane, of the sufferings of the crew:

Our dried penguins began to corrupt, and there bred in them a most loathsome and ugly worm of an inch long. . . . [T]here was nothing that they did not devour [including] our clothes, boots, shoes, hats, shirts, stockings: and for the ship they did so eat the timbers, as that we greatly feared they would undo us. . . . The more we labored to kill them, the more they increased; so that at the last we could not sleep for them, but they would eat our flesh and bite like mosquitoes. In this woeful case . . . our men began to fall sick of a monstrous disease. . . . Divers grew raging mad, and some died in most loathsome and furious pain.

Richard Hakluyt, *Principal Navigations*

Left **This nineteenth-century engraving depicts the arrival of the English at Roanoke in 1587; this settlement was the second of two unsuccessful attempts, promoted by Hakluyt, to found an English colony in America. One member of the landing party holds up a cross as a statement of intent to introduce English Protestantism to the American Indians.**

SEE ALSO

- Northeast Passage • Northwest Passage • Raleigh, Walter

HANNO OF CARTHAGE

HANNO OF CARTHAGE made one of the earliest recorded European journeys of exploration beyond the Mediterranean Sea, sometime around 500 BCE. Having set sail from his home town, the Phoenician colony of Carthage on the northern coast of Africa, Hanno undertook a remarkable journey along the West African coast, during which he was attacked by strange creatures, saw a volcanic eruption, and encountered native African peoples.

Right **This map depicts the probable route of Hanno's voyage beyond the Pillars of Hercules (the Straits of Gibraltar) and along the coast of West Africa.**

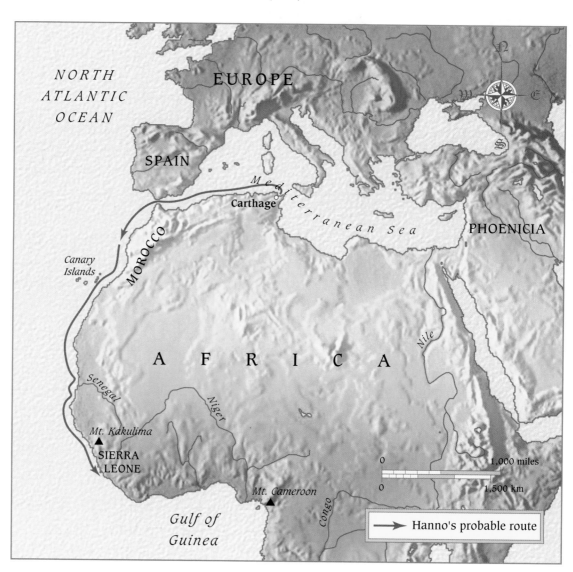

Other than a later translation of Hanno's eighteen-line account of his journey, no historical evidence of Hanno's life remains. Most scholars agree that Hanno's voyage probably took him as far as present-day Sierra Leone, but it is possible that he circumnavigated the entire African continent.

HANNO'S JOURNEY

According to his account, Hanno's enormous fleet comprised sixty ships and 30,000 men. After setting sail from Carthage, he followed the African coastline, first to the west alongside present-day Morocco and then to the south toward the equator. Under orders to

Masters of the Sea

By the time of Hanno, the Phoenicians' seafaring skills had helped them to establish a network of trading posts, including several silver mines in Spain and along the African coast. An important innovation around the time of King Sennacherib (705–681 BCE) was the bireme. With oarsmen placed on two levels, double the number of rowers could fit in a ship of a given length. The trireme, with oarsmen on three levels, followed shortly after.

establish more Carthaginian trading posts, he dropped off teams of colonists as he went.

At one stage of his journey south, Hanno became friendly with a nomadic tribe and took interpreters aboard. Farther on, men clad in animal skins threw stones at Hanno's men, and the crew was unable to go ashore. At least ten days after they had left Carthage, Hanno's ships reached a wide river, "teeming with hippopotami and crocodiles" (it is thought to be the Senegal River).

After nineteen more days of sailing, Hanno reached a great gulf, which his translators called the "Horn of the West." Four days later they passed an erupting volcano that

Below **Hanno encountered a great deal of exotic wildlife, including primates that may have been gorillas, chimpanzees, or baboons. The Roman historian Pliny (23–79 CE) relates that the animals' furs were displayed in the temple of the goddess Tanit at Carthage.**

spewed "torrents of fire" into the sea. Three days later he reached the "Horn of the South" before returning home.

DID HANNO CIRCUMNAVIGATE AFRICA?

Conservative estimates claim that the volcano Hanno encountered was Mount Kakulima in Guinea, but many scholars identify it as Mount Cameroon, which lies over two thousand miles (3,200 km) farther along the coast. Some experts believe that, as winds and tides would have made it difficult for Hanno to sail back to Carthage the same way he came, it would have been easier for him to continue in the same direction and thus sail around the whole continent. The Roman historian Pliny the Elder (first century CE) stated that Hanno was under orders to circumnavigate Africa and that he reached "the extremity of Arabia." According to the earlier Greek historian Herodotus (480–425 BCE), the Phoenicians had already circumnavigated Africa in the seventh century BCE.

DID HANNO FIND GORILLAS?

Hanno describes an encounter in the Horn of the South with creatures with hairy bodies. His men attempted to capture them, but the creatures threw stones at their captors and bit and scratched them. Eventually the creatures were killed and skinned.

Hanno recorded his impression of the name local tribesmen gave the animals: *gorilla*. He may have heard the words *ngò dìida*, which in the Kikongo language mean "powerful animal that beats itself violently."

The creatures now known as gorillas were named in the eighteenth century because of Hanno's account. However, gorillas do not throw stones, and their response to being carried off is likely to be more violent than biting or scratching. It is possible that the animals Hanno saw were chimpanzees or baboons.

Hanno's journey was full of incident:

. . . we continued for five days along the coast, until we reached a great bay which according to our translators was the Horn of the West. . . . Here we disembarked. In daytime, we could see nothing but the forest, but during the night, we noticed many fires alight and heard the sound of flutes, the beating of cymbals and tom-toms, and the shouts of a multitude. We grew afraid and our diviners advised us to leave this island. Quickly and in fear, we sailed away from that place. Sailing on for four days, we saw the coast by night full of flames. In the middle was a big flame, taller than the others and apparently rising to the stars. By day, this turned out to be a very high mountain, which was called Chariot of the Gods.

Hanno, *Periplus*, 14–16

THE *PERIPLUS* OF HANNO

Hanno's account of his travels was inscribed on tablets, which he dedicated to the Phoenician god Melqart and placed in a temple. A Greek visitor to Carthage in the fifth century BCE jotted down a translation, which in turn was copied several times by Greek and Roman scribes. The journal was given the name *Periplus* (literally, "sailing around").

The account is remarkable for several reasons. It is the longest known text written by a Phoenician author. Moreover, it is the only firsthand report of West Africa before the logbooks of the Portuguese explorers, written two thousand years later. Though only eighteen lines long, it is a fascinating and unique insight into early exploration.

SEE ALSO
• Portugal • Ships and Boats • Tides and Currents

HENRY THE NAVIGATOR

WITH HIS CAREFULLY PLANNED program of exploration along the western coast of Africa, Prince Henry of Portugal (1394–1460), later called "the Navigator," did more than any other individual to launch the great European Age of Discovery. Within fifty years of his death, the process that Henry began would see Portuguese ships sailing to India, Southeast Asia, Brazil, and the Pacific Ocean.

HIGH AND MIGHTY CONQUESTS

Henry the Navigator was the younger son of King John I of Portugal. At his birth a court astrologer cast Henry's horoscope. According to the royal chronicler, the astrologer predicted that Henry was destined to work "at high and mighty conquests, especially in seeking out things that were hidden from other men." Henry grew up believing that his destiny was to fulfil this prophecy.

Henry made his first conquest when he was twenty-one. In August 1415 he sailed with an invasion fleet to North Africa, where he took part in the capture of the Muslim city of Ceuta (in present-day Morocco). All his life Henry would see himself as a crusader, a Christian soldier engaged in fighting a holy war against the forces of Islam. He considered the Muslims who ruled North Africa and southern Spain to be the "enemies of God."

GOVERNOR OF THE ALGARVE

In 1419 John I made Henry the governor of the Algarve, the southernmost province of Portugal. The following year Henry also became Grand Master of the Order of Christ, the Portuguese brotherhood of crusaders. Henry set up his own court at Sagres, where he developed a powerful war fleet of caravels, small ships with lateen (triangular) sails. Each year Henry sent his caravels to raid Muslim strongholds on the African coast. Information gathered on these raids formed the basis of subsequent exploration of the African coast.

Below **This man, his hands clasped in prayer, has been identified as Henry the Navigator. He stands behind the young king, Afonso V (bottom right), in a group portrait of the Portuguese royal family painted in the 1460s.**

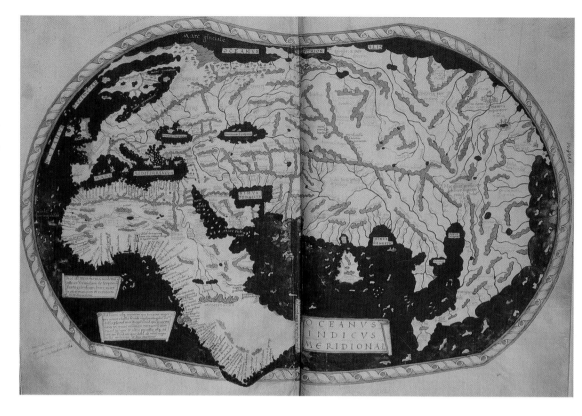

Right **This famous world map was drawn around 1490 by the German cartographer Henricus Martellus. It is one of the first maps to portray the Portuguese discoveries along the coast of West Africa.**

Muslim caravans loaded with gold dust and ivory frequently arrived in North Africa, having traveled across the Sahara Desert from the African interior. The Portuguese concluded that Africa contained great wealth, but they knew little of the continent beyond a point six hundred miles (966 km) south of Sagres called Cape Non (*non* is French for "no"). Superstitious sailors chose this name because they believed nobody could sail past this cape and return alive.

Henry decided to send his ships past Cape Non to discover the source of Africa's wealth, which he could then use to pay for his wars against the Muslims. His plan was to send young noblemen from his own court, rather than sea captains, to lead voyages of exploration. The prince knew that sailors were too cautious to sail into unknown waters and that the knights and squires of Henry's court were born risk takers who lived for warfare and adventure. To such men a voyage into the unknown was a heroic quest that might win them lasting glory.

One of Henry's goals was to find Prester John, a legendary Christian priest-king who was thought to live somewhere in Africa or Asia. Henry dreamed that he and the mighty Prester John would form a military alliance and drive the Muslims out of Africa.

1415
Prince Henry takes part in the capture of Ceuta, North Africa.

c. 1420
João Gonçalves Zarco and Tristão Vaz Teixeira rediscover Madeira.

c. 1427
Portuguese sailors make their first voyages out of sight of land and rediscover the Azores.

1434
Gil Eannes sails past Cape Bojador, the edge of the known world, on his second attempt.

1440s
Henry sends colonizing fleets to the Azores.

1441
Nuno Tristão reaches Cape Blanc.

1444
Six caravels carrying African slaves return to Portugal.

1445
Dinis Dias reaches the Senegal River and rounds Cape Vert.

1455–1456
Usodimare and Cadamosto explore the Senegal and Gambia Rivers and sight the Cape Verde islands.

1460
Henry's captain Pedro de Sintra reaches the coast of Sierra Leone; Henry dies on November 13.

HENRY'S DISCOVERIES

Henry's campaign of exploration began in the 1420s, when his ships navigated a safe route past Cape Non. In the same year an expedition led by João Gonçalves Zarco and Tristão Vaz Teixeira rediscovered Madeira, an island in the Atlantic Ocean. The island was given its name because it is heavily forested (*madeira* means "wood" in Portuguese). The island had considerable commercial appeal for Portugal, a country in which timber was a scarce resource. From about 1425 Portuguese settlers colonized Madeira and began to cut down the trees.

Prester John

Rumors of a mighty Christian king in central Asia named Prester John had fascinated Europeans since the twelfth century, when a letter supposedly written by the priest-king to the rulers of Europe was widely circulated. Over time, stories of Prester John's wealth and power grew ever more exaggerated. According to Sir John Mandeville, the purported author of a fourteenth-century collection of travelers' tales, the realm of Prester John lay somewhere in Africa. Mandeville wrote that the priest-king ruled over seventy-two other kings, each of whom had kings under them, and that his army of 110,000 warriors marched to battle behind tall gold crosses covered in jewels. An inscription on a 1460 world map by Fra Mauro, cartographer to the Venetian court, estimated Prester John's army as a million strong.

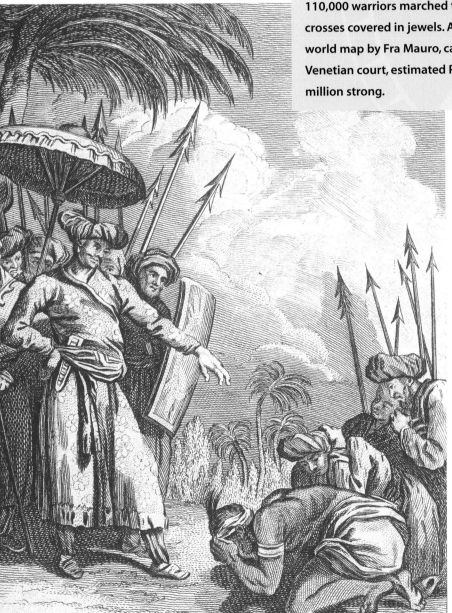

Left **This engraving depicts Prester John, the legendary Christian priest and king of the Middle Ages, with his defeated enemies kneeling before him. Despite the absence of supporting evidence, in various forms the legend of Prester John persisted into the late seventeenth century.**

Above **In this painting Henry displays a map of his discoveries and is surrounded by the mapmakers, navigators, and captains of his court. In their hands and around the room are navigational instruments, a sword, and a model of a caravel.**

Henry's next goal was to pass Cape Bojador on the northwestern coast of the Sahara, a point that had replaced Cape Non as a barrier in the minds of superstitious sailors. For twelve years the crews of the caravels refused to sail past this cape. Cape Bojador was finally rounded in 1434 by Henry's shield bearer, Gil Eannes, on his second attempt, and Cape Blanc, even farther south, was reached by another of Henry's captains, Nuno Tristão, in 1441.

From the 1440s on, Henry sent settlers, many of them convicts, to the Azores, an island group in the Atlantic that one of Henry's expeditions had reached in 1427. Meanwhile, in 1445 Dinis Dias reached the Senegal River and the Cape Vert promontory.

Slaves

In the 1440s Henry's captains began to capture Africans, at first to learn about the country and later to bring them home to sell as slaves. Henry, in common with many of his contemporaries, saw nothing wrong in enslaving Africans. He believed that he was helping them, for they would be taught Christianity—which Henry considered the true faith. The royal chronicler Zurara wrote of these slaves, "though their bodies might be in a state of servitude, that was small matter when compared with the fact that their souls would enjoy true freedom for ever."

The Africans, who saw the matter very differently, fought back. In 1446 twenty Portuguese sailors were killed while raiding a village. The Portuguese learned that it was much safer to trade with local chiefs for slaves rather than capture slaves themselves. Slavery was already well established in Africa, and the chiefs were eager to exchange captives caught on raids for Portuguese cloth, horses, and trinkets, such as brass bells. The European trade in Africans, started by Henry, would last for the next four centuries.

African Rivers

The final significant voyages sent out by Henry were led by two Italian explorers, Antonio di Usodimare and Alvise da Cadamosto. In 1455 and 1456 the two men explored the lower reaches of the Gambia and Senegal Rivers, two of West Africa's great waterways. Cadamosto's account of these journeys contains fascinating information about the Africans. He wrote, for example, that when Africans first saw Portuguese ships, they believed them to be "great sea birds with white wings, which were flying and had come from some strange place."

On August 6, 1444, the first Portuguese slaving fleet of six caravels unloaded its cargo in Lagos, southern Portugal. Henry supervised the proceedings, mounted on a horse. An eyewitness, the chronicler Zurara, described the slaves' behavior:

Some held their heads low, their faces bathed in tears as they looked at each other; some groaned very piteously . . . others struck their faces with their hands and threw themselves full length on the ground. . . . [It was] necessary to separate sons from their fathers and wives from their husbands. . . . As soon as the children who had been assigned to one group saw their parents in another, they jumped up and ran towards them; mothers clasped their children in their arms and lay face downwards, accepting wounds . . . rather than let their children be torn from them.

Gomes Eanes de Zurara, *The Chronicle of Guinea*

SEE ALSO

• Portugal

HEYERDAHL, THOR

Below **This photograph of Thor Heyerdahl dates from 1958, when** *Aku Aku,* **an account of his trip to Easter Island, was published.**

THOR HEYERDAHL (1914–2002) was a Norwegian explorer, anthropologist, and author. In a series of pioneering expeditions, he tested his theories about how early people may have crossed the world's oceans and demonstrated how ancient technology and natural materials could be used to make primitive but still effective oceangoing vessels.

PEOPLING THE PACIFIC ISLANDS

Thor Heyerdahl was born on October 6, 1914, in Larvik, southeastern Norway. While studying zoology and geography at Oslo University, Heyerdahl developed an interest in the remote islands of the Pacific Ocean. In 1937, before he graduated, Heyerdahl traveled to Fatu Hiva, a Polynesian island in the Marquesas group, situated midway between Australia and South America.

As Heyerdahl observed the people of Fatu Hiva, he began to wonder where their ancestors had come from. In the 1930s anthropologists thought the original inhabitants of the Pacific islands had migrated from Southeast Asia, but Heyerdahl came up with a different theory. Noting that the ocean currents flowed from east to west, he proposed that the Pacific islands had been first settled by people from South America. The Fatu Hiva islanders seemed to preserve a distant memory of this event in their story of a god named Kon-Tiki, whom they said had brought them to Fatu Hiva from an ancestral land that lay far to the east.

1914
Thor Heyerdahl is born in Larvik, Norway.

1937–1938
Lives on Fatu Hiva, a Polynesian island.

1947
Crosses the Pacific Ocean on the *Kon-Tiki.*

1952–1953
On the Galápagos Islands, finds pre-Columbian pottery from Peru.

1955–1956
On Easter Island, finds evidence of early contact with South America.

1970
Crosses the Atlantic Ocean on the *Ra II.*

1977–1978
Crosses the Indian Ocean on the *Tigris.*

1982–1984
Conducts archaeological excavations on the Maldive Islands.

1988–1994
Conducts excavations at Túcume, Peru.

2002
Dies at Colla Michari, Italy.

THE *KON-TIKI* EXPEDITION

Although many anthropologists refused to accept his theory, Heyerdahl was convinced of it and put it to the test in a famous experiment. In 1947 he and five companions sailed west from Peru on a raft named *Kon-Tiki*. Built from balsa wood and bamboo, it was the type of vessel Heyerdahl believed had made the Pacific crossing centuries earlier. For 101 days the raft was carried by the wind and tides across five thousand miles (8,000 km) of sea until it reached Raroia, an island east of Tahiti. Heyerdahl had provided dramatic evidence that people from South America could once have made such a journey.

THE *RA* AND *TIGRIS* EXPEDITIONS

In 1970 Heyerdahl crossed the Atlantic Ocean from Morocco in North Africa to Barbados in the Caribbean Sea on *Ra II*, a raft made from papyrus reeds. *Ra II* was forty feet (12 m) long, had a crew of eight, and was a replica of an ancient Egyptian reed boat. Its fifty-seven-day journey demonstrated that in ancient Egypt the materials and technology had existed to construct oceangoing craft.

Heyerdahl describes the huge physical effort needed to steer the *Kon-Tiki*:

We clung like flies, two and two, to the steering oar in the darkness, and felt the fresh sea water pouring off our hair while the oar hit us till we were tender both behind and before, and our hands grew stiff with the exertion of hanging on. . . . When we were tired out with pushing the oar we went over to the other side and pulled, and when arms and chest were sore with pressing, we turned our backs, while the oar kneaded us green and blue in front and behind.

Thor Heyerdahl, *The Kon-Tiki Expedition*

Below **Heyerdahl constructed *Kon-Tiki* (pictured here sailing on the Pacific Ocean) from locally available balsa logs at Callao, Peru, and in three and a half months traversed some five thousand miles (8,000 km) of ocean. The *Kon-Tiki* has been preserved in a museum in Oslo, Norway.**

Right **The *Ra II*, a boat made using materials and technology available to ancient Egyptians, being towed through the streets of Cairo, Egypt, in 1969. From Cairo it was taken to Morocco, where it began a 3,500-mile (5,600 km) journey across the Atlantic Ocean to Barbados.**

Heyerdahl saw his Atlantic crossing as evidence that contact could have been made between the peoples of the Mediterranean region and those of Central and South America long before either the Norsemen or Christopher Columbus crossed the Atlantic.

Heyerdahl's last sea adventure, in 1977, was on another reed boat, the eleven-man *Tigris*, a

Heyerdahl the Archaeologist

Heyerdahl directed a number of archaeological excavations. On the Galápagos Islands he found artifacts of Peruvian origin, and on Easter Island (Rapa Nui) he demonstrated that the original inhabitants may have traveled there from South America, 2,300 miles (3,700 km) to the east. He also excavated at Túcume, northern Peru, where he discovered a stone frieze, carved about 1100 CE, depicting reed boats—a find that further hints at the possibility of long-distance ocean travel in ancient times.

fifty-foot (15 m) copy of an ancient Sumerian craft. His plan was to demonstrate how the cultures of ancient India, Egypt, and Mesopotamia could have been in contact with each other by sea. The vessel sailed from Iraq along the Tigris River through the Persian Gulf and into the Indian Ocean, but at Djibouti the expedition was brought to a halt by war in the Horn of Africa. Heyerdahl burned the *Tigris* in protest at the region's wars and at the pollution of the sea that he had witnessed on the way.

In re-creating the sea journeys that ancient people may have made, Heyerdahl demonstrated that there are considerable gaps in historical knowledge about the early exploration of the world. His pioneering work changed understanding of how the islands of the Pacific may have been peopled. Heyerdahl died on April 18, 2002, at his home in Italy.

SEE ALSO

• Scandinavia

• Ships and Boats

HILLARY, EDMUND

THE MOUNTAINEER AND EXPLORER Edmund Percival Hillary was born in Auckland, New Zealand, in 1919. On May 29, 1953, together with a Sherpa climber named Tenzing Norgay, Hillary became the first man known to have reached the summit of Mount Everest, at 29,035 feet (8,850 m) the highest point in the world. Between 1955 and 1958 Hillary took part in the Commonwealth Trans-Antarctic expedition, which reached the South Pole in January 1958. His later years have been devoted to the welfare of the Sherpa, a people of Tibetan descent who live in Nepal.

After leaving Auckland Grammar School, Edmund Hillary made a living as a beekeeper and served in the New Zealand Air Force. He spent much of his spare time climbing mountains and in 1949 took part in the first ascent of the southern ridge of Mount Cook, New Zealand's highest peak. In 1951 he was invited to join an expedition to the Indian Himalayas and later that year took part in the British reconnaissance expedition to Mount Everest. The aim of the expedition was to find a route to the peak of the world's highest mountain.

EVEREST EXPEDITION

In 1953 Colonel John Hunt was appointed to lead the well-organized and well-equipped British Everest Expedition. The team reached South Peak by the beginning of May and was on schedule to reach the summit of Everest before the onset of the monsoon snows. First Charles Evans and Tom Bourdillon attempted to reach the summit, but the strain of climbing at high altitudes exhausted them and forced them to turn back. Next it was the turn of Hillary and Tenzing Norgay, who had experienced seven Everest expeditions between them (but had never climbed together). Camping on ice at 27,900 feet (8,503 m), the two men had an evening meal of chicken noodle soup, sardines, dates, and apricots and tried to rest before the final assault on Everest.

Below **In his memoirs Hillary confessed that his "solar plexus was tight with fear" as he approached the summit of Everest. His achievement earned him a knighthood in 1953.**

The two men left their forward camp on the south col in the freezing chill of dawn on May 29, 1953. Five hours later they became the first men known to have reached the summit. Tenzing left gifts of food there for the gods of the great mountain. The conquest of Everest was announced to the world on the morning of the coronation of the young Queen Elizabeth II. The triumph of the British Everest expedition added to the public celebrations. Hillary was knighted for his heroic achievement. Tenzing received the George Medal, Britain's highest civilian award for bravery.

EXPEDITION TO THE ANTARCTIC

Now famous throughout the world, Hillary looked to the Antarctic for a new challenge. The Commonwealth Trans-Antarctic Expedition (1955–1958) aimed to make the first mechanized crossing of the continent. Expedition leader Vivian Fuchs would set off from one side, while Hillary would lead a team of New Zealanders from the other. In January 1958 Hillary and his comrades, traveling in a convoy of specially designed tractors, became the first men to reach the South Pole overland since Roald Amundsen and Robert Scott in 1911 and 1912, respectively.

Right **Having reached the South Pole by snowtractor on January 3, 1958, Hillary met up with the rest of the Commonwealth expedition, led by Sir Vivian Fuchs (pictured right).**

1919
Edmund Hillary is born in New Zealand.

1951
Takes part in reconnaissance expedition to Everest.

1953
With Tenzing Norgay, makes the first known ascent of Mount Everest.

1958
Reaches South Pole overland by tractor from the Ross Ice Shelf.

1960
Leads expedition to the Himalayas to find evidence of the abominable snowman.

1961
Establishes Himalayan Trust.

1985
Is appointed New Zealand High Commissioner to India and Nepal.

Climbing Chomolungma

The world's highest mountain, known in Nepal as Sagarmatha, in Tibet is called Chomolungma, which means "goddess mother of the world." The English name commemorates a British officer, George Everest, who surveyed India and the Himalayas in the middle of the nineteenth century. As Nepal was for a long time closed to foreigners, Everest remained a mysterious mountain in the minds of Europeans. British surveyors first calculated its height at 29,002 feet (8,840 m) in 1856. The earliest mountaineering expeditions by British teams in 1921 and 1922 reached the unprecedented height of 27,297 feet (8,320 m) on the northeast ridge.

The ill-fated 1924 British expedition made the headlines in newspapers around the world. Climbing without additional oxygen, Edward Norton and Howard Somervell almost reached the top but were forced back when they were only about a thousand feet (300 m) from the top. However, it was the mysterious death of George Mallory and Andreas Irvine on this expedition that caught the world's attention. To this day historians of mountaineering wonder if they managed to reach the summit, thanks to their use of modern oxygen bottles, before falling to their death on the way down. Later expeditions between 1933 and 1951 also failed owing to the extreme altitude and terrible weather conditions that guard the world's highest peak.

Above **Everest (left) is the highest of a group of peaks that includes the sharp Nuptse (right).**

THE HIMALAYAN TRUST

In 1960 Hillary returned to the Himalayas on an expedition to search for the abominable snowman, a mythical monster believed by some people to live in the mountains. Hillary was deeply fond of Nepal and its people but was aware that this small, poor country faced many social and economic problems. In 1961 he set up the Himalayan Trust with the aim of helping the people of Nepal. Since 1961 the trust has helped to build over thirty schools, twelve health clinics, and two major hospitals. In 1985 Hillary's affection for the Nepalese people was recognized when he was appointed New Zealand High Commissioner for India, Nepal, and Bangladesh.

SEE ALSO

• Great Britain

HIPPARCHUS

THE GREEK ASTRONOMER AND MATHEMATICIAN Hipparchus (c. 190–c. 120 BCE) lived for much of his life on the Mediterranean island of Rhodes, where he spent years drawing up an analysis of the stars that was to prove invaluable to later explorers. Hipparchus also calculated the length of the solar year and was the first person to locate accurately the positions of places on earth with reference to lines of latitude and longitude.

Above **This engraving of Hipparchus looking through a telescope (first used around 1600) is anachronistic.**

Few details of Hipparchus's life remain. He was born about 190 BCE in the city of Nicaea (present-day Iznik in northwestern Turkey). At some point he moved to the island of Rhodes, off the southwestern coast of Turkey.

It was on Rhodes that Hipparchus devoted his life to science, and for this reason he is often known as Hipparchus of Rhodes (though he is also referred to as Hipparchus of Nicaea, after the town of his birth).

c. 190 BCE
Hipparchus is born at Nicaea (present-day Iznik), Turkey.

c. 134 BCE
Observes a new star in the constellation of Scorpio and formulates the principle that the stars are not fixed in the heavens.

c. 129 BCE
Completes his catalog of about 850 stars.

c. 120 BCE
Dies, probably at Rhodes.

HIPPARCHUS THE ASTRONOMER

On Rhodes, Hipparchus spent years observing the night sky and noting the positions and movements of the stars and planets. He made his observations with the naked eye as well as with new astronomical instruments of his day,

The Armillary Sphere

*T*he armillary sphere was invented by the Greeks, probably during the second century BCE, and it remained the standard instrument of astronomical observation until the invention of the optical telescope in the seventeenth century CE. The armillary sphere was a model of the universe (then thought to have the earth at its center) and was composed of connected metal rings, usually six, that moved around a small terrestrial globe.

After aligning the sphere's outermost ring with the horizon, the astronomer sighted an inner ring on a star whose position was known. Once the armillary sphere was thus "fixed" in place, the astronomer could then make observations of the heavens in order to record the positions of other celestial bodies in relation to one another.

Below This armillary sphere, made in 1648, is similar to the type used by Hipparchus seventeen hundred years previously.

such as the armillary sphere and the plane astrolabe. He spent many years in Rhodes, where, in about 129 BCE, he produced the world's first known star catalog, which records the position and relative brightness of around 850 stars.

Hipparchus based his observations of the stars on the position of the equinoxes, the two imaginary points in the sky where, twice a year, the path of the sun crosses the celestial equator (an imaginary continuation of the plane of the earth's equator in the heavens). When Hipparchus compared his observations with those made by Babylonian astronomers and by Timocharis, a Greek astronomer who worked about 280 BCE, he discovered that, instead of remaining in the same position in the night sky, the equinoxes appeared to have moved slightly. This phenomenon, known as the precession of the equinoxes, occurs because the earth's axis of rotation is not fixed in space but slowly follows a circular path that takes fully 26,000 years to complete. If the earth's rotation were speeded up, the planet would appear to wobble slightly. Hipparchus's discovery enabled later astronomers to build a more accurate picture of the universe. Navigators used the new astronomical knowledge to plot a course with greater precision.

HIPPARCHUS THE MATHEMATICIAN

Hipparchus's observation of the night sky led him to compute a table of numbers, known to the Greeks as chords. From the chord table developed the science of trigonometry, a branch of mathematics concerned with the properties of triangles, and so it is often said that Hipparchus was the originator of trigonometry. However, Hipparchus considered trigonometry not as a branch of mathematics but as a function of astronomy, since for him it was purely a means to calculate the positions of stars and other celestial bodies.

Hipparchus's skills as a mathematician enabled him to make an accurate estimate of the length of the solar year, which he calculated as 365 days, 5 hours, 55 minutes, 12 seconds—only about 6 minutes in error according to present-day calculations. He calculated the length of the lunar month (from new moon to new moon) as 29 days, 12 hours, 44 minutes, 2.5 seconds—less than a second away from the figure accepted by modern scientists.

Another measurement made for the first time by Hipparchus was the distance of the moon from the earth, which he calculated as approximately 250,000 miles (402,000 km). The actual distance is around 239,000 miles (385,000 km). Hipparchus based his calculation of this figure on data recorded during a total eclipse of the sun that occurred on March 19, 190 BCE.

HIPPARCHUS THE GEOGRAPHER

Hipparchus's work as an astronomer and mathematician greatly increased understand-

Below **The astrolabe, which may have been invented by Hipparchus, was used by astronomers and navigators to calculate the time at night by measuring the positions of the stars.**

ing of the position of earth in the universe; his work as a geographer greatly increased understanding of the physical nature of the earth itself.

Hipparchus knew about the world map drawn up by Eratosthenes (c. 276–c. 194 BCE), the first map to use a grid system to plot the locations of physical features. However, he criticized Eratosthenes' map because the grid was irregular and the position of its physical features had not been plotted according to astronomical measurements. Hipparchus used trigonometric calculations to devise alternative projections of the world that would allow for the curvature of the earth's surface. He was the first person to attempt map projections that took into account the distorting effect of representing the curved earth on a flat surface and the first to fix places on the earth by coordinates of latitude and longitude, a method that is still a vital component of cartography. However, despite the fact that it improved on existing ways of mapmaking, Hipparchus's method was not adopted by cartographers until some two hundred years after his death.

Hipparchus died sometime around 120 BCE. He described his life's work in many books, which, with the exception of one, have all been lost. Luckily, Greek and Roman writers who read his books referred to them in their own works, and thus what is known about Hipparchus comes from their accounts. Two hundred years after his death, the Greek astronomer and geographer Claudius Ptolemy (c. 90–c. 168 CE) was particularly influenced by the work of Hipparchus, whom he called "the lover of truth."

Hipparchus the Inventor

*I*t is thought that a measuring device known as the plane astrolabe was invented by Hipparchus. Consisting of a bronze disk with a movable chart of the night sky, the plane astrolabe enabled an astronomer to make calculations of the rising and setting of celestial bodies and thus to reach an accurate estimation of the time at night. The instrument could also be used to measure angles. The astrolabe only became obsolete with the invention of the sextant, more than 1,800 years after Hipparchus's death.

SEE ALSO

- Astronomical Instruments • Astronomy
- Eratosthenes of Cyrene
- Latitude and Longitude • Ptolemy

Houtman, Cornelis

CORNELIS HOUTMAN (1540–1599) was one of the first Dutch explorers to travel to the East Indies (present-day Malaysia, Singapore, and Indonesia). Houtman's two journeys, on which he was accompanied by his brother Frederik (1570–1627), established the first trade contact between those islands and the Netherlands. These contacts eventually led to the foundation of the Dutch East India Company, which in the seventeenth century became a dominant force in the global spice trade and helped the Netherlands to enjoy a period as one of the world's most powerful trading nations.

Right **Although this portrait of Cornelis Houtman bears his intials and his signature, the date and artist are unknown.**

TRADING RIVALS

The Netherlands first began to turn its attention to the East Indies during the 1590s. At this time the lucrative spice trade was dominated by the Spanish and Portuguese, whose expeditions were financed and controlled by the royal families of those countries. Dutch exploration, on the other hand, was strictly an entrepreneurial matter: it was funded by private companies set up by groups of merchants.

SPIES

In 1592 one such company of nine merchants sent Cornelis and Frederik Houtman to Lisbon, the Portuguese capital, to investigate the workings of Portuguese trade in the East Indies. The brothers were arrested and charged with attempting to steal secret Portuguese shipping charts of southeastern Asia. They were convicted and imprisoned for three years.

1540
Cornelis Houtman is born in Gouda in the Netherlands.

1592
Cornelis and Frederik are imprisoned in Lisbon.

1595
Having returned to Amsterdam, the brothers set sail for the East Indies on April 2.

1596
The brothers establish trade contact with Java, Sumatra, and Bali, and return to Amsterdam with a cargo of spices.

1598
They embark on a second voyage, in which they establish trade with Madagascar.

1599
Cornelis Houtman is killed in a battle with the sultan of Aceh (Sumatra).

VOYAGE TO THE EAST INDIES

When the brothers were released in 1595, they returned to Amsterdam. Aiming to establish themselves in the East Indies, the nine merchants had by this time formed the Compagnie van Verre (literally, "long distance company"). During his time in Lisbon, Cornelis had learned a great deal about the spice trade, and the Verre Company appointed him commander of an expedition of four ships.

The brothers set sail on April 2, 1595, and faced difficulties from the outset. Of the 249 men who set out, seventy-one had died of scurvy by the time the ships reached the Indian Ocean. This disease, caused by a lack of vitamin C, was common on naval journeys during the sixteenth and seventeenth centuries, when little fresh food was available. Its Dutch name, *scheurbuik*, means "tearing stomach." The Houtmans were forced to stop in Madagascar, an island off the east coast of

Below **This painting depicts a Dutch fleet returning home from the East Indies in 1599.**

The Spice of Life

Dutch merchants lost a lot of money on Houtman's first voyage, but their investment paid off in the early sixteenth century when the Dutch took control of the East Indies spice trade. Spices were used in Europe to preserve and flavor meat and to make medicines and perfumes. They were ideal trade goods as they were easy to handle and large quantities could be broken up into smaller portions for sale. However, spices grew only in southern and southeastern Asia. Popular spices included cinnamon from Sri Lanka, nutmeg and cloves from the Moluccas, ginger from China, and pepper from the islands of present-day Indonesia. Because they were so difficult to obtain, spices were expensive: a Dutch word for something whose price is excessively high is *peperduur*—as expensive as pepper.

Right **During the seventeenth century the bustling Amsterdam shipyard of the Dutch East India Company was the engine room of the world's most powerful commercial organization. Although his voyages laid the foundations of the Dutch spice trade, Houtman never lived to see the outcome.**

Africa, where one of the bays became known as the Hollandsche Kerckhoff (Dutch cemetery). During the voyage Houtman was engaged in almost daily quarrels with his chief merchant, Meulenaer, and the captain of one of his ships, Gerrit van Beuningen. These disputes caused serious rifts among the crew members, who grew restless and fought among themselves.

THE EAST INDIES

In 1596 the ships arrived in the port of Bantam on the island of Java. Houtman found a much larger Portuguese presence—both merchants and soldiers—than he had been

expecting. The movement of spices was entirely in the hands of the Portuguese, and Houtman had to work hard to establish contact with local tribal leaders. He met with hostility wherever he went, from Portuguese traders resenting the presence of a rival and from local tribes unwilling to deal with another European power.

THE RETURN JOURNEY

After Houtman had visited Sumatra and Bali, two principal islands of the East Indies, he prepared to return to the Netherlands. The journey home was as tough as the outward one had been. Beyond the Cape of Good

Frederik Houtman 1570–1627

Frederik Houtman survived the 1599 battle in which his brother was killed but was captured and imprisoned. During his confinement he studied the Malay language. When he returned to Amsterdam after his release in 1602, he wrote the first Malay-Dutch dictionary. This book was an important tool for merchants of the newly founded Dutch East India Company as it began to establish itself in Southeast Asia. From 1605 to 1611 Frederik Houtman served as governor of the new Dutch territory of Amboina, in the Moluccas, and from 1621 to 1623 he was governor of the whole province of the Moluccas (a group of islands that is now part of Indonesia).

In the middle of the night on July 29, 1619, Frederik Houtman was sailing off the western coast of Australia when his ships came upon two small sandy islands lying just above the surface of the water. At high tide they disappeared from view, and an unwary navigator might find his ship beached sixty miles from the coast. For this reason Frederik named the islands Houtman's Abrolhos—the Portuguese word *abrolho* literally means "open your eyes."

SECOND VOYAGE

In 1598 Cornelis and Frederik Houtman were hired once more, this time by an Amsterdam merchant named de Moucheron, who wanted to explore the possibility of trade between the Netherlands and the East Indies. Once again, Houtman had to deal with a restless crew and was greeted with hostility by natives of the islands he visited. In September 1599, on the island of Sumatra, Cornelis and his crew were attacked by the forces of the sultan of Aceh. Some historians claim that the Portuguese, unwilling to share the spoils of the spice trade with another power, encouraged the sultan to attack the Dutch. Many members of the expedition, including Cornelis Houtman himself, were killed.

Hope, the Atlantic Ocean was under the control of the Portuguese, and the Dutch ships were unable to stop anywhere between southern Africa and Amsterdam.

Houtman and his exhausted crew, reduced to eighty-nine men, returned home on August 14, 1597, with a small cargo of pepper. They had obtained much less from the islands than the Verre Company had expected.

Although Houtman did not have much to show for his efforts in material terms, he had proved that the Portuguese did not have a stranglehold on the spice trade. Dutch merchants and explorers were soon able to take advantage of Houtman's pioneering voyage.

SEE ALSO

- Illness and Disease • Netherlands • Portugal
- Spain

HUDSON, HENRY

Below **This idealized engraving shows Indians welcoming Henry Hudson in 1609 as he explores the North American river later named after him.**

THE ENGLISH SEAFARER HENRY HUDSON (c. 1570s–1611) was one of the most accomplished navigators of the seventeenth century. He made four voyages in search of a northern sea route to Asia and explored three great North American bodies of water—a strait, a bay, and a river—that were later named after him. Hudson is also remembered for the terrible way in which he met his death.

MAY 1607
On his first voyage, Henry Hudson searches for a route over the North Pole to China.

SEPTEMBER 15, 1607
Returns to England.

APRIL 22, 1608
Departs in search of a northeast passage.

JUNE 26, 1608
Reaches Novaya Zemlya.

AUGUST 26, 1608
Returns to England.

MARCH 25, 1609
Sails northeast from Amsterdam in the *Half Moon*.

MAY 19, 1609
Heads west across the Atlantic.

SEPTEMBER 3–OCTOBER 4, 1609
Explores the Hudson River.

NOVEMBER 7, 1609
Returns to England.

APRIL 17, 1610
Sails from London on his fourth voyage.

AUGUST 3, 1610
Sails into Hudson Bay.

NOVEMBER 10, 1610–JUNE 18, 1611
Discovery is frozen in the ice.

JUNE 21–22, 1611
Discovery's crew mutinies; Hudson, his son, and seven others are set ashore in northern Canada, where they die.

SAILING DUE NORTH

Nothing is known of Henry Hudson's life until 1607, when he was employed by the London-based Muscovy Company of Merchants to find a sea route to China by sailing due north over the Pole. On May 1 Hudson sailed from London in a small ship called the *Hopewell*. His crew of eleven included his young son John, who would accompany him on all his journeys. After a difficult voyage, Hudson reached 80°23' north latitude, about 1,357 miles (2,184 km) from the North Pole, where his ship was in danger of being driven onto the ice and wrecked. Fortunately, a wind rose up and blew the ship to safety. "If not for the deliverance by God," wrote Hudson, "it would have been the end of us and our voyage." He returned to London with the news that it was not possible to sail over the North Pole.

HEADING NORTHEAST

In April 1608 Hudson made a second voyage in the *Hopewell*, his goal this time being to find a northeast passage to Asia by sailing across the seas north of Russia. He reached the islands of Novaya Zemlya but was again prevented from continuing by ice. Concluding that there was no northeast passage, Hudson wrote, "I thereby resolved to use all means I could to sail to the northwest."

A DUTCH VOYAGE

After two unsuccessful voyages the Muscovy Company was unwilling to send Hudson on a third, and so he approached the Dutch, England's greatest trading rival. The Dutch agreed to back another voyage to the northeast, and although Hudson agreed, he seems to have intended secretly to sail west.

On March 25, 1609, Hudson sailed from Amsterdam in the *Half Moon*. By mid-May the crew of twenty sailors, both Dutch and English, had grown to dread the intense cold

On June 15, 1608, Hudson recorded in his journal a strange sight two of his crew members claimed to have witnessed:

This morning, one of our crew while looking overboard saw a mermaid, calling the rest of the crew to come see her. One more came up; by that time she was close to the ship's side and looking earnestly at the men. . . . As they saw her, from the navel upward, her back and breasts were like a woman's, her body as big as ours, her skin very white, and she had long, black hair hanging down behind. In her going down they saw her tail, which was like the tail of a porpoise, and spotted like a mackerel.

Quoted in Donald Johnson, *Charting the Sea of Darkness*

and Arctic storms. Fearing a mutiny, Hudson persuaded his crew to join him on an expedition westward. He crossed the Atlantic and reached Nova Scotia in July 1609. He then followed the coast south and entered what is now New York Harbor. He was greatly excited at discovering the wide Hudson River, thinking that it might be the sought-after passage through America to the Pacific. Hudson sailed upstream about 150 miles (241 km) but turned back when he found the river growing too shallow. He returned to England, where the government ordered him to make no further voyages for the Dutch.

LAST VOYAGE

Convinced that the passage he was seeking lay in the far northwest, Hudson soon set sail on a new voyage. He was backed by a small group of rich London merchants, who gave him command of the *Discovery*, with a crew of twenty-two.

The *Discovery* crossed the Atlantic and on July 5 reached the passage of water now called Hudson Strait. A month later, the ship entered Hudson Bay, a large landlocked area of water that Hudson must have believed to be the Pacific Ocean. Sailing south, he expected to find the warmer waters of the Pacific but instead reached an anchorage and before long found himself trapped in the ice at the foot of the bay.

For six months the men were stuck on their icebound ship. Supplies of fresh food soon ran short, and the crew began to suffer from scurvy, a disease caused by a shortage of vitamin C. Hudson caused great resentment by seeming to favor certain members of the crew over the rest. Some thought that he was secretly hoarding food and giving it to his favorites while leaving the others to starve.

Right **Like many seventeenth-century explorers, Hudson entered the straits of northeastern Canada in search of a northwest passage to Asia but found only a series of landlocked bays.**

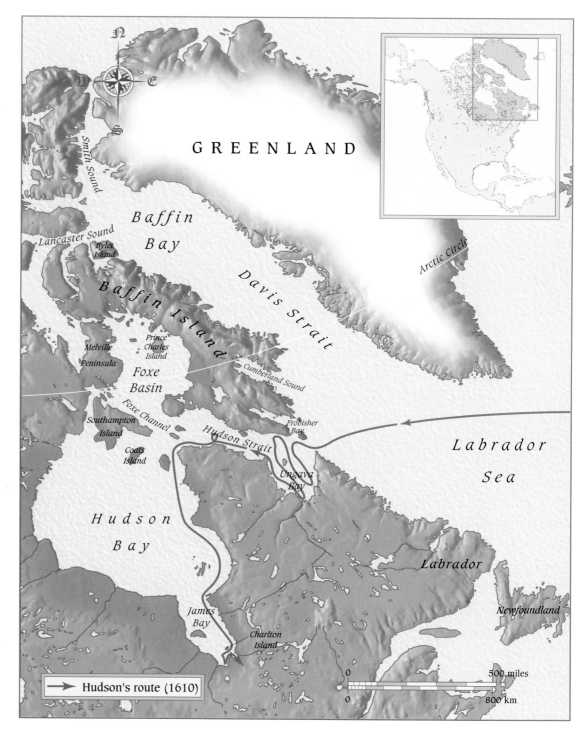

Hudson's route (1610)

Hudson's Fate?

Nicolas de Vignau, one of Samuel de Champlain's men, spent the winter of 1611 and 1612 among the Algonquins. Later he told Champlain he had traveled north to Hudson Bay and seen the wreck of an English ship. He had heard stories that, when the ship's crew raided a Cree encampment for food, the Cree cut off the men's heads but spared a boy. The only English in the area in 1611 were the eight men set adrift by the mutineers, including Hudson and his son. However, when Champlain got to the Algonquins in 1613, they denied that de Vignau had traveled north with them.

In mid-June, when the ship was finally freed from the ice, a mutiny broke out, led by Robert Juet, William Wilson, and Henry Greene. Greene argued that he "would rather be hanged at home than starved abroad." On the morning of June 22, they seized Hudson as he came out of his cabin and tied him up. He was put into the ship's boat with his son, four sick men, and three who remained loyal to him. Then the mutineers sailed away, leaving them to their fate.

The *Discovery* returned to London, manned by just eight survivors of the voyage. Four mutineers, including Wilson and Greene, had been killed in a fight with Inuit (members of a people native to Canada and Greenland), while Juet had died of starvation on the way home. The survivors were tried for murder by the Admiralty Court but escaped punishment by putting the blame for the mutiny on those who had died.

Above **Hudson's terrible fate appalled and fascinated later writers and artists, including the painter of this 1907 work.**

SEE ALSO
- Baffin, William • Cabot, Sebastian
- Northeast Passage • Northwest Passage

HUMBOLDT, ALEXANDER VON

THE GERMAN NATURAL SCIENTIST AND EXPLORER Alexander von Humboldt (1769–1859) is often considered the father of modern geography. Having written that "the most dangerous view of the world is that held by those who have never really viewed the world," Humboldt spent five years (1799–1804) collecting huge amounts of information on the animals, plants, people, and physical geography of South and Central America, an area that had never before been studied in depth. Among many other achievements, Humboldt made science more popular, set up a worldwide network of observatories, and even broke the world mountain-climbing record.

Right **Humboldt's writings and lectures made him a celebrity in his own lifetime and did much to popularize science.**

EARLY LIFE

It was as a nineteen-year-old student of engineering in Berlin that Alexander von Humboldt first began to show a flair for science. He developed a passion for botany and began collecting and classifying specimens from the surrounding countryside.

In 1789 Humboldt became interested in the earth sciences. He studied mineralogy and geology at the University of Göttingen and continued his education at the newly established School of Mines in Freiberg. In 1792 he was a given a job at the Prussian Mining Department and was sent to the remote Fichtel Mountains, where he supervised all mining of gold and copper and gained a reputation for tireless hard work. He invented a safety lamp and set up a mining school before he became convinced that his aim in

---

1769
Humboldt is born in Berlin.

1789–1790
Spends a year at the University of Göttingen.

1790
Joins the School of Mines in Freiberg.

1792
Supervises gold and copper mines in the Fichtel Mountains.

1799–1804
Undertakes a major exploration of the Spanish colonies in Central and South America.

1804–1827
Lives in Paris and dedicates much of his time to publishing the data collected on the expedition.

1827
Returns to Berlin.

1836
Persuades the British government to set up observatories throughout the world to study magnetic storms.

1845–1858
The first four volumes of *Kosmos*, one of the greatest works of popular science, are published.

MAY 6, 1859
Humboldt dies in Berlin while working on the fifth volume.

life was scientific exploration. In 1797 Humboldt resigned his position and began to look for an expedition.

VOYAGE TO SOUTH AMERICA

In 1799 Humboldt was given special permission by King Charles IV of Spain to join an expedition to the Spanish colonies in Central and South America, which were usually out of bounds to non-Spaniards. He set sail from Marseilles in the summer of 1799 in the company of Aimé Bonpland, a French botanist. During a grueling five-year journey, Humboldt and Bonpland covered six thousand miles (9,650 km) on foot, by canoe, and on horseback and made a strikingly large number of discoveries. Starting in Venezuela, Humboldt and Bonpland sailed up the Casiquiare River and proved that the great Orinoco and Amazon river systems were

Aimé Bonpland *1773–1858*

Aimé-Jacques-Alexandre Goujaud Bonpland was a physician by profession, and after his medical studies in Paris, his first voyage was as a ship's surgeon. However, he developed a keen interest in plants and joined Humboldt in the quest to collect scientific information from unexplored parts of the world.

Bonpland accompanied Humboldt on his five-year journey in Venezuela, Colombia, Peru, Ecuador, Mexico, and the United States. During their voyage, Bonpland collected and classified around 60,000 plants, 6,300 of them previously unknown. He published his findings in *Plantes equinoxiales* between 1806 and 1810.

Bonpland and Humboldt shared more than a voyage—both have had a geographical feature on the moon named in their honor: the Bonpland crater and Mare Humboldtianum, a sea.

Below **Humboldt and Bonpland traveled up the Guayas River in Ecuador on the raft depicted in this drawing.**

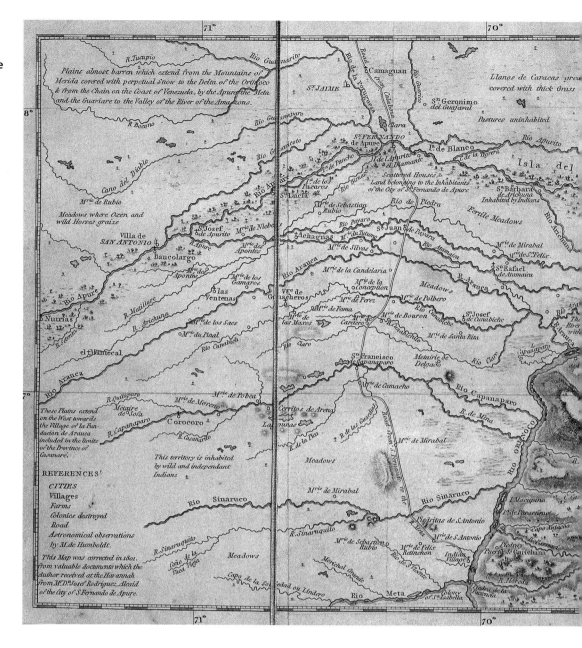

Right **This map shows the part of the province of Verina between the Orinoco, Apure, and Meta Rivers. It was published in the second volume of Humboldt's *Personal Narrative of Travels to the Equinoctial Regions of the New Continent during the Years 1799–1804.***

connected. After three months in the rain forest, their supplies were destroyed by insects and rain, and they were forced to live on beans and river water.

The two explorers then followed the Andes Mountains from Colombia to Peru and observed the effects of different altitudes on plants and animals. Humboldt climbed almost to the top of Chimborazo, an extinct volcano. His ascent to 19,280 feet (5,877 m) remained unequaled for thirty years. He noted that the mountain sickness from which he suffered was due to a lack of oxygen in the air at high altitudes.

A WEALTH OF DATA

Humboldt returned to Europe in 1804 with an abundance of new information. He had observed and collected thousands of specimens, including the electric eel, a startling creature in an age when electricity itself was a mystery. His depiction of measurements of temperature and atmospheric pressure on weather maps laid the foundations for the science of climatology. He noted the medical importance of the cinchona plant, whose bark can cure malaria. His drawings of Incan ruins in Peru proved invaluable for later chroniclers of that civilization.

The Humboldt Current

*I*n 1802 Humboldt discovered a current of water off the coast of Peru about 550 miles (900 km) wide, with a temperature five to ten degrees lower than the waters surrounding it. The Humboldt Current (now known as the Peru Current) is caused by winds that blow parallel to the coast of South America and take away the warm surface of the water. The current brings fog to the coast of Peru, yet the winds make this area one of the driest places in the world. It also encourages the growth of tiny plankton, which provide nourishment for large quantites of fish, and thus the waters off Peru are one of the world's greatest fishing grounds for anchovy and tuna.

geomagnetic field. Determined to establish for certain whether magnetic storms were of terrestrial or extraterrestrial origin, in 1836 he persuaded the British government to set up observatories in its territories throughout the world, including Canada, South Africa, Australia, and New Zealand. The project was one of the first examples of international scientific collaboration, and its findings led to the discovery that magnetic storms were caused by sunspots and thus were of extraterrestrial origin.

KOSMOS

From 1827 until a few years before his death, Humboldt served as tutor to the crown prince of Prussia. He gave popular public lectures and organized scientific conferences. In 1845 the first volume of *Kosmos*, an account of the structure of the universe, was published. In the 1850s three more volumes of *Kosmos* appeared. The purpose of this lengthy and ambitious work was to find "unity in the vast diversity of phenomena ... from the nature of the nebulae down to the geography of the mosses clinging to a granite rock." Humboldt died in 1859, at the age of ninety, while working on the fifth volume.

WRITING UP HIS NOTES

It took Humboldt twenty-five years to complete publication of his and Bonpland's findings, in more than thirty lavishly illustrated volumes. A shorter version, in three volumes, became a best-seller and was an inspiration for the young Charles Darwin, who took a copy with him aboard the *Beagle* in 1831.

MAGNETIC STORMS

During his trip to South America, Humboldt had become interested in magnetic storms—sudden fluctuations in the earth's

SEE ALSO

- Darwin, Charles
- Geography
- Natural Sciences

IBN BATTUTAH

THE ISLAMIC SCHOLAR IBN BATTUTAH (1304–1369) has been called the greatest traveler of all time. He left his home in Morocco and crossed North Africa to visit the holy city of Mecca (in present-day Saudi Arabia). From there, his travels over the next thirty years took him some 75,000 miles (120,000 km), from Africa to China and to almost every Muslim country in the world.

Right **Ibn Battutah's travels during the fourteenth century took him to every Islamic country in the known world.**

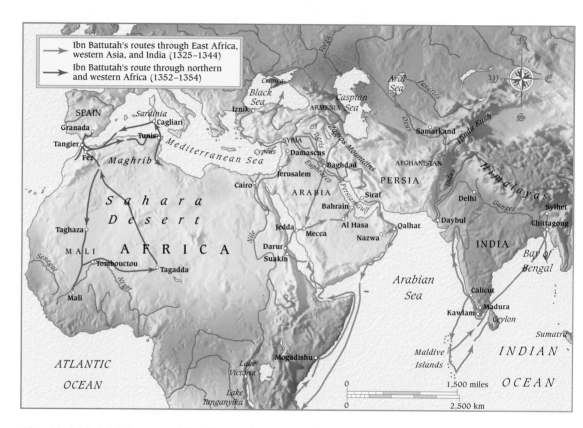

Abu Abd Allah Muhammad ibn Battutah was born in Tangier, Morocco, in 1304. When he was twenty-one, he made his first hajj (pilgrimage) to the Muslim holy city of Mecca.

The hajj is a journey that all devout Muslims are expected to make once in their life; for Ibn Battutah it marked the beginning of a lifelong quest to discover more about the Islamic

1304
Ibn Battutah is born in Tangier, Morocco.

1325–1327
Makes his first pilgrimage to Mecca in Arabia and then travels through Syria, Palestine, and Persia.

1327–1330
Returns to Mecca to study Islamic law. Travels to Yemen and along East African coast.

1330–1332
Travels to Asia Minor (present-day Turkey), Crimea (southern Russia), and Afghanistan.

1333–1345
Explores the Indus valley in India and works for the sultan of Delhi. Visits Maldive Islands, Ceylon, and Burma.

1346–1349
Sails to China via Sumatra. Travels home to Morocco via Calicut (India), Oman, Baghdad, and Cairo.

1349
Visits the kingdom of Granada.

1352–1354
Traveling across the Sahara, spends one year in the kingdom of Mali.

1355–1356
Returns to Morocco and dictates his memoirs to a scribe at the court of Sultan Abu Inan.

1369
Dies in Tangier.

world, a quest that would cover over 75,000 miles (120,000 km).

The Travels of Ibn Battutah

On his first journey Ibn Battutah crossed North Africa, passing through Egypt and Syria before arriving in Arabia. In Mecca he paid the traditional visit to the Great Mosque and walked seven times around the Kaaba, a sacred black stone. His description of this first visit shows the fervor of a deeply religious man: "he who embraces it wishes never to cease embracing it."

Ibn Battutah traveled throughout Syria and Persia before returning to Mecca, where he spent a further three years. After this second stay in the holy city, he traveled down the east coast of Africa before journeying north through Arabia and Syria, across the Black Sea and into Russia. From there he crossed the Hindu Kush Mountains into Afghanistan before journeying on to India. He spent many years traveling through India and worked as a legal adviser to the sultan of Delhi until 1345, when he was sent as the sultan's ambassador to China. He traveled there via the Maldive Islands and Ceylon (present-day Sri Lanka) before sailing around the Bay of Bengal. By 1347 he was back in India, and in 1348 he returned to Mecca before journeying home to Morocco.

Although Ibn Battutah had been traveling for nearly twenty-five years, he still wanted to see more Muslim countries. He traveled to the kingdom of Granada in Spain, and on his final adventure, starting in 1352, he crossed the Sahara Desert, where he stayed with nomadic tribes, and visited the kingdom of Mali.

Years of Adventure

During his travels Ibn Battutah not only developed a deep knowledge of the Islamic world but also had exciting adventures and

The Dhow

Ibn Battutah traveled the sea routes used by Arab traders as a passenger on a type of ship called a dhow, a long, light wooden vessel with triangular sails and a short mast. Strong enough to withstand storms and monsoon rains, dhows carried large cargoes of silk, spices, and other exotic goods from the East.

Above **Ancient dhows, such as the one pictured in this medieval manuscript, were made from wooden planks tied together with palm tree fronds.**

faced many dangers. He often traveled with a band of people, including friends, servants, scholars, and wives. He evaded being kidnapped, survived shipwrecks, and was once forced into marriage. He was respected and well looked after by many of his hosts. While in India he was welcomed into several royal households. He claimed that he was pre-

Right **Ibn Battutah
visited Egypt in 1325
and again in 1348; in
this engraving, a local
guide is showing him
the ruins of a temple.**

sented with horses and even entire villages as gifts. For a few years he stayed at the court of Sultan Muhammad ibn Tughluq, who asked Ibn Battutah to lead a royal envoy (a diplomatic mission representing the sultan) to China.

Ibn Battutah enjoyed observing how other cultures lived and worked. In China he became interested in the ancient art of porcelain manufacture. He also admired the Chinese use of paper money rather than gold. During his stay in Damascus, Syria, he was impressed that poorer Muslims were given money to make their pilgrimage to Mecca. He praised the people of the Sahara for their justice and honesty.

Ibn Battutah did not admire everything he encountered: he was offended by the naked women he saw in Tombouctou in the Sahara. He sometimes made errors in his observations: when he saw hippopotamuses for the first time, he thought they were elephants.

Ibn Battutah's account of his epic journey is generally known as the *Rihlah (Travels)*. As well as describing his many adventures, the book contains political, social, and cultural observations and includes useful information on such practical matters as roads, caravan routes, inns, and navigation. One of the first travel books ever written, it provides a unique record of life in the Islamic world in the fourteenth century.

MEMOIRS

Ibn Battutah returned to Fez in Morocco in about 1355. While at the court of Sultan Abu Inan, he began dictating his memoirs to the scribe Ibn Juzay. It is said that it took three months to recount his adventures. Ibn Battutah injected wit into his descriptions of everyday life and had a keen eye for detail. Recounting his time in Baghdad, he noted the excellent bathing facilities. He described how each bather was presented with three towels: "one to wear round his waist when he goes in, another to wear round his waist when he comes out, and the third to dry himself with."

Ibn Battutah describes the Indian love of betel leaves:

Betel trees are grown like vines on can trellises or else trained up coco-palms. They have no fruit and are grown only for their leaves. The Indians have a high opinion of betel, and if a man visits a friend and the latter gives him five leaves of it, you would think he had given him the world, especially if he is a prince or notable. A gift of betel is a far greater honor than a gift of gold and silver. It is used in the following way: First one takes areca nuts, which are like nutmegs, crushes them into small bits and chews them. Then the betel leaves are taken, a little chalk is put on them, and they are chewed with the areca nuts.

The Travels of Ibn Battutah

Left **Ibn Battutah landed in the Chinese port of Zayton, described by Marco Polo as one of the great ports of the East. During his journey inland to Peking, he became fascinated by porcelain manufacture, shown here on wallpaper made during the Qing dynasty (1644–1912).**

SEE ALSO

- Idrisi, al-Sharif al-
- Polo, Marco

IDRISI, AL-SHARIF AL-

Below **As a student in Cordoba, Spain, al-Idrisi would have worshiped at the stunning eighth-century Great Mosque.**

REMEMBERED AS ONE OF THE GREATEST of medieval mapmakers, al-Idrisi was born in Morocco in 1099 and died in Sicily in 1165. Although there is little historical evidence of the details of his life, his fame was secured by the remarkable maps, including a map of the world, that he produced for King Roger II of Sicily.

THE ARAB EMPIRE

Abu Abd Allah Muhammad ibn Muhammad al-Idrisi was born in Ceuta, Morocco, and educated at the University of Cordoba in southern Spain. Cordoba, because of its position in the west of the Islamic Empire, was a meeting place for different cultures. As an Islamic scholar al-Idrisi traveled throughout Arabia. He also traveled to northern Europe, visiting France and England—an unusual thing for a Muslim of his day to do.

In 1099 the Islamic world stretched from India to Spain and included many different countries, states, and tribes. To govern and maintain order in such a vast empire, Muslim leaders required a sound knowledge of geography. Indeed, all Muslims required a basic geographical awareness in order to make the hajj (pilgrimage) to the holy city of Mecca, which Islam requires its followers to do at least once in their life. Finally, an understanding of where places were and the routes that connected them was vital for the merchants and traders who transported goods throughout the empire.

For centuries Arabs had gathered information about different regions and the routes between different places. They had studied ancient maps, including those of the ancient Greek geographer Ptolemy, and added their own information about the world to new maps and charts.

1099
Al-Idrisi is born in Ceuta, Morocco.

1154
Completes the *Book of Roger* for King Roger II of Sicily.

1161
Completes a second book, *The Gardens of Humanity and the Amusement of the Soul* for King William I of Sicily.

c. 1165
Dies in Sicily.

1192
The atlas known as the *Little Idrisi* is produced.

Ibn Khordadhbeh c. 850 CE

When al-Idrisi was writing and creating his maps in the twelfth century, he was partly inspired by a writer who had lived nearly two hundred years earlier. Ibn Khordadhbeh was a civil servant from Iran who, in 846, wrote *The Book of Roads and Provinces*. In his book Ibn Khordadhbeh gave details of roads, caravan routes, rivers, and deserts. He enlivened this practical information with descriptions of people and buildings.

TRAVELERS' TALES

The journals written by Arab travelers during the Middle Ages were both geographical (they contained maps and information about routes and features) and ethnographical (they provided descriptions of the people who inhabited various parts of the world). Although these books were intended primarily as educational tools, they were read by Arabs for enjoyment as well. For people in the West, who had little or no knowledge of life in the Arab world, they were an invaluable source of information. Several Christian monarchs of Europe welcomed Muslim intellectuals into their court as consultants on aspects of life in the Muslim countries.

After a long period of travel, al-Idrisi himself was welcomed into the court of Roger II (1097–1154), the Norman king of Sicily. At that time Islam and Christianity were political enemies. Between 1066 and 1071 the Christian Normans had reconquered Muslim Sicily. Islamic strongholds in southern Italy and throughout the Mediterranean were threatened by further Christian invasions. By taking up residence in a recently conquered land, al-Idrisi was seen as a traitor by many Muslims. It may be for this reason that so little information about him has survived.

Roger II was already a collector of Arab geographical works when he summoned al-Idrisi to his court to help produce a map of the world. The two men worked closely together and employed a team of educated men to travel abroad and gather information about the places to be included in their map, including their longitude and latitude, the distance between them, and their social and cultural background. For over fifteen years al-Idrisi compiled the travelers' data, continually updating information he had already gathered as new reports came in.

WONDERS OF THE WORLD

In his encyclopedia of geography, completed in 1154, al-Idrisi declared that the earth was spherical, with a circumference of about 22,900 miles (36,850 km). He described regions of Asia, Africa, and Europe and included information on the oceans and weather. He named his work *The Book of Roger*, after the king who commissioned it.

In that same year, 1154, al-Idrisi crafted two magnificent objects for the king, considered at the time to be wonders of the world: a small silver planisphere (a representation of

Below **On al-Idrisi's world map of 1154, south is at the top, and the Arabian peninsula can be clearly identified in the center.**

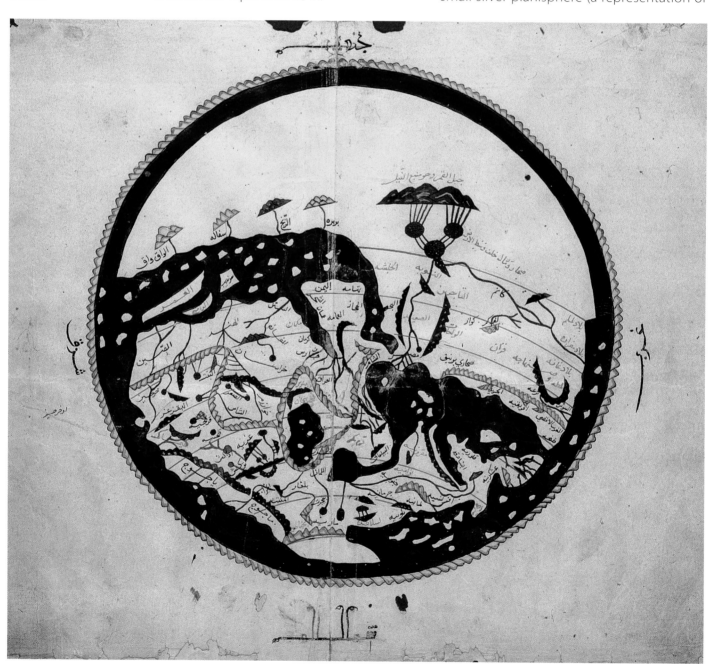

the spherical earth on a flat surface) and a large silver tablet engraved with a map of the world. The tablet, which probably measured 12 feet (3.6 m) by 5 feet (1.5 m), was destroyed in 1160.

A few weeks before Roger's death in 1154, *The Book of Roger* was translated into Latin and Arabic, and the maps were reproduced on seventy sheets of paper.

AL-IDRISI'S ATLAS

After Roger's death al-Idrisi is thought to have compiled a more detailed journal, in the style of Ibn Khordadhbeh, for Roger's son, King William I. *The Gardens of Humanity and the Amusement of the Soul* was published in 1161, but no copy of it remains. It is thought that al-Idrisi died in 1165, though historians are not certain of the date.

In 1192 a selection of al-Idrisi's writings and seventy-three of his maps were compiled in an atlas that is now known as *Little Idrisi*. Although al-Idrisi had not managed to plot the world accurately, he had produced one of the best representations of the world of his time. He had also managed to compile all the geographical knowledge of the era in a single work. Despite this achievement al-Idrisi was not widely read in medieval times. By the time *Little Idrisi* was translated into Latin in Rome in 1619, it was more of a curiosity for students of geography than an influential piece of work.

LEGACY

As well as for his achievements in geographical scholarship, al-Idrisi is recognized for his contribution to botany and research into medicinal plants. He updated information about plants that had not been studied since the time of the ancient Greeks. Through his research he discovered the medicinal properties of plants that had never been used in remedies before.

Al-Idrisi describes the lost city of Ghana in northern Africa:

. . . the most considerable, the most densely peopled, and the largest trading center of the Negro countries. . . . From the town of Ghana, the borders of Wangara are eight days' journey. This country is renowned for the quantity and the abundance of the gold it produces. It forms an island 300 miles long by 150 miles wide: this is surrounded by the Nile on all sides and at all seasons. . . . The greater part [of the gold] is bought by the people of Wargalan and by those of Western Maghrib [Morocco].

Al-Idrisi, *Little Idrisi*

Above **Al-Idrisi's richly colorful map of the Red Sea, found in a manuscript published in 1182, includes the towns of Medina and Mecca.**

SEE ALSO

• Ibn Battutah • Ptolemy

ILLNESS AND DISEASE

MANY EXPLORERS SUFFERED from illness on their journeys. Europeans, in particular, died by the thousand from diseases such as scurvy, dysentery, and malaria. In view of the horrible sufferings that explorers endured as a result of illness and disease, it is remarkable that any of them ever left home at all.

Below **The English admiral George Anson lost more than a thousand men to scurvy on a voyage around the world in the 1740s.**

THE SCOURGE OF THE SEA

The single greatest cause of death among explorers was scurvy, a disease brought about by a deficiency of vitamin C. The only natural source of this vital nutrient is fresh fruit and vegetables; as such foods cannot be stored for long periods without rotting, scurvy was extremely common on long expeditions in areas where fresh supplies of fruit and vegetables were impossible to find. Explorers succumbed to scurvy in places as diverse as the icy wastes of the Arctic and the hot dry deserts of Australia, but the disease struck most commonly on long voyages by sea.

The greatest disaster caused by scurvy took place on a voyage around the world, from 1740 to 1744, led by the English naval commander George Anson. All of the crew came down with the disease, and out of 1,950 men, only 700 survived. By the final stages of the voyage, Anson was throwing fifteen bodies a day into the sea.

1499
Vasco da Gama loses thirty men to scurvy while returning home from the Indian Ocean.

1519–1530
Smallpox, brought by Europeans, sweeps through the Caribbean and Central America.

1520–1521
Ferdinand Magellan's fleet is devastated by scurvy while crossing the Pacific.

1596
Francis Drake dies of dysentery on board his ship in the Caribbean.

1604–1605
Wintering in Canada, Samuel de Champlain loses 35 of his 79 men to scurvy.

1740–1744
During George Anson's voyage around the world, 1,250 men die from scurvy.

1794
British navy begins to issue lime juice to sailors.

1816
James Tuckey dies of malaria while exploring the Congo River in Africa.

1820
Quinine is extracted from the cinchona bark.

1857–1858
John Speke and Richard Burton search for the source of the Nile.

1873
David Livingstone dies in Africa of dysentery.

1899
Robert Peary loses eight toes to frostbite

1912
On their return from the South Pole, Robert Scott and his party die of hypothermia.

Anson's officers had plenty of opportunity to observe the disease, and they made detailed descriptions of its symptoms. The commonest symptoms of scurvy were swollen gums, blackened limbs, and great loss of bodily strength. Scurvy sufferers also tended to become emotionally disturbed and were easily terrified by the slightest upset. A sufferer in the last stages of scurvy might die of shock at a loud noise, such as the firing of a ship's cannon. Perhaps the most peculiar effect of scurvy was that the disease made old wounds, apparently healed, open up again. According to one story, an old sailor on Anson's voyage, who had been wounded more than fifty years previously at the Battle of the Boyne (1690), was amazed when his old battle scars broke open and formed fresh wounds.

Pascoe Thomas, a schoolmaster who sailed with Anson, subsequently described his own experience of scurvy:

I was first taken . . . with a small pain on the joint of my left toe . . . in a little time a large black spot appearing. . . . Many more black spots appeared . . . accompanied with . . . excessive pains in the joints. . . . It next advanced to my mouth; all my teeth were presently loose, and my gums, overcharged with . . . blood, fell down almost quite over my teeth. This occasioned my breath to stink much . . . I believe, one more week at sea would have ended me.

From Pascoe Thomas's journal

Below **British sailors on the 1875 expedition to the Arctic of HMS *Alert* were issued lime juice to prevent scurvy. Despite this precaution, many men fell ill from the disease during the long Arctic winter.**

The Anson disaster forced the British navy to concentrate on solving the problem of scurvy. Many remedies were tried. On the voyage of the *Endeavour* to the South Pacific (1768–1771), Captain James Cook gave his men pickled cabbage and malt. Because none of his crew died from scurvy, Cook was convinced that these foods had prevented the disease. In fact, pickled cabbage and malt are not high in vitamin C, and the survival of his men was due more to luck and to the frequent landfalls Cook made, when he had the opportunity to take on supplies of fresh vegetables and fruit.

The problem of scurvy at sea was finally solved in the 1790s, when the British navy began to issue a daily ration of lemon or lime juice to sailors. Yet the cause of the disease was not fully understood until 1932, when the existence of vitamin C was discovered.

The White Man's Grave

For European explorers, the most feared and deadly diseases were those encountered in Africa. It is for this reason that Africa was also referred to as the "white man's grave."

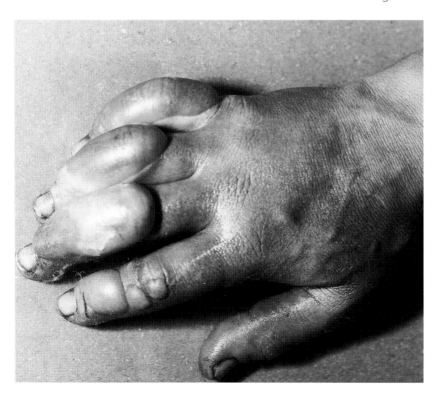

Below **These blisters are the symptoms of superficial frostbite, in which ice crystals form in the skin. More deadly is deep frostbite— dreaded by polar explorers—which can freeze muscles, veins, and even bone.**

Mosquitos transmitted malaria and other fevers, while tsetse flies carried fatal sleeping sickness. Gut infections, which resulted from drinking dirty water, caused typhoid fever and dysentery. Other horrible diseases included river blindness and elephantiasis, in which the legs swell up so much that they resemble those of an elephant.

There survive few tales of an explorer's suffering to compare with that of John Hanning Speke, who took part in an 1858 expedition to search for the source of the Nile River. At one point a beetle crawled into his ear and began to dig away at his eardrum. Speke, desperate to remove the beetle, stuck a penknife in his ear and killed the beetle but wounded the ear so badly that infection set in. As a result the left side of his face became covered in boils, and he could not open his mouth for a week.

Speke also suffered from a mysterious illness, the symptoms of which he described as akin to being branded with a hot iron in various parts of his body. Suffering from fever and writhing in agony, he temporarily went out of his mind. According to his companion, Richard Burton, he suddenly sat up and "began to utter a barking noise, and a peculiar chopping motion of the mouth and tongue, which so altered his appearance that he was hardly recognizable."

Diseases of the Cold

The Arctic and the Antarctic are the coldest and perhaps most hostile places on earth. The commonest danger of the extreme cold, made worse by the biting wind, is frostbite, which occurs when skin and underlying tissues freeze, usually on the face, feet, or hands. Unless circulation is restored to the affected area, the tissues die and begin to decay, a condition called gangrene, and the only treatment is to remove the affected area. Many polar explorers lost toes to frostbite.

Quinine

*F*rom the seventeenth century, the Spanish in South America were treating themselves for fevers with the bark of the cinchona tree, a remedy they had learned from the Indians. In 1820 two French chemists extracted a medicine they named quinine from this bark. Quinine lowers the body temperature and can also kill the malaria parasite. Traveling in Africa between 1841 and 1873, the explorer David Livingstone suffered repeatedly from malaria and other fevers. The fact that he survived for over thirty years in the so-called white man's grave was due to quinine.

Left This nineteenth-century engraving depicts Peruvian Indians demonstrating to European travelers the medicinal properties of cinchona bark, from which quinine—the first effective treatment for malaria—is extracted.

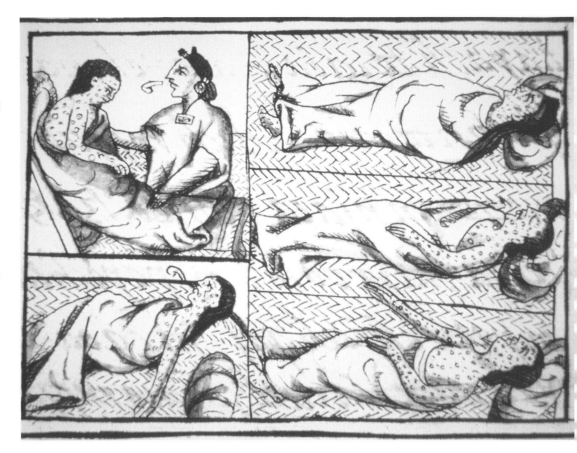

Right **This illustration, from a Mexican manuscript, shows Aztecs succumbing to smallpox, a disease that was brought to the Americas in 1521 by the Spanish conquistadores. The Aztec account reads, "We were covered with agonizing sores from head to foot. The illness was so dreadful that no one could walk or move."**

Returning from their journey to the South Pole in 1912, Captain Robert Scott and his sledging party suffered from frostbite. One of the men, Oates, had such badly frostbitten feet that he could no longer keep up. Rather than hold his companions back, he walked out of the tent to his death in a blizzard.

In 1899 Robert Peary lost eight toes to frostbite on a midwinter expedition across Ellesmere Island, in the Canadian Arctic. His companion, Matthew Henson, removed Peary's sealskin boots:

He ripped the boots from both feet and gently removed the rabbit-skin undershoes. Both legs were a bloodless white up to the knee and, as Matt ripped off the undershoes, several toes from each foot clung to the hide and snapped off at the first joint.
"My God, Lieutenant! Why didn't you tell me your feet were frozen?" Matt cried.
"There's no time to pamper sick men on the trail," Peary replied . . . "Besides, a few toes aren't much to give to achieve the Pole."

Bradley Robinson, *Dark Companion*

Despite Oates's sacrifice, the other men died from scurvy, starvation, frostbite, and hypothermia, which occurs when the body loses so much heat that it can no longer function.

DISEASES CARRIED BY EXPLORERS

From the time of the first voyage of Christopher Columbus in 1492, Europeans brought diseases to the Americas never before encountered by the native peoples, including smallpox, influenza, measles, chicken pox, and the common cold. Illnesses that were mild in Europe were often deadly to Native Americans. It has been estimated that up to 90 per cent of the Native American population was wiped out by diseases borne by Europeans in the hundred years after the arrival of Columbus.

SEE ALSO

- Burton, Richard Francis • Livingstone, David
- Peary, Robert E. • Polar Exploration
- Speke, John Hanning

JOLLIET, LOUIS

BORN IN NEW FRANCE (the French colonies of North America) in 1645, Louis Jolliet was part of the first company of white men to explore the Mississippi River. Jolliet and fellow explorer Jacques Marquette concluded—correctly—that the river emptied into the Gulf of Mexico. Jolliet also explored Canada's eastern coast before he died in 1700.

EARLY LIFE

As a young man, Louis Jolliet considered entering the priesthood, but he later decided to become a fur trader. At the age of twenty-two, he spent a year in France studying hydrography (the science of bodies of water). He returned to North America and quickly gained a reputation as an explorer and trader.

DOWN THE MISSISSIPPI

In 1670 Jean-Baptiste Talon was reappointed intendant of New France. The intendant was second in command to the governor and had responsibility for the colony's economic development. Talon asked Jolliet to head an expedition to a great river, known from Indian reports, that lay to the west of the Great Lakes. Jolliet's task was to find this river and to determine whether it flowed south into the Gulf of Mexico or west into the Pacific. As a reward Jolliet would be permitted to trade along the way. In May 1673 Jolliet set out with a Jesuit priest named Jacques Marquette and five companions.

Traveling in canoes, the men paddled from Lake Michigan to Green Bay, where they entered the Fox River. From the Fox they portaged (carried their canoes overland) to the Wisconsin River, which they followed southwest to the Mississippi. They took the Mississippi past its junctions with the Ohio and Missouri Rivers. Just before they reached the mouth of the Arkansas River, they turned back. Convinced that the Mississippi flowed into the Gulf of Mexico, they were afraid of capture by Spanish forces farther south.

Left **In this picture Jolliet and Marquette are shown using the shallow-riding canoes of Native Americans to explore the Mississippi River. In reality, the explorers would never have stood up in a canoe, for fear of capsizing or of puncturing the birch bark with the pressure of their shoes.**

Right **This seventeenth-century French map reflects the discoveries of Jolliet and Marquette. The Mississippi River is shown, left of center, flowing down to the Gulf of Mexico.**

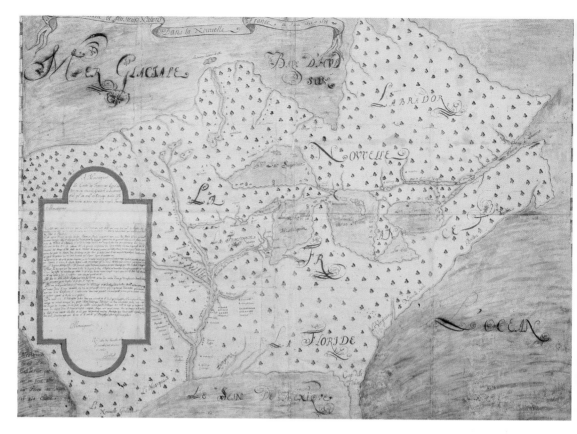

During the winter Jolliet worked on journals and maps describing the voyage. Unfortunately, these papers were lost when his canoe was overturned in rapids on the way back to Montreal. He later re-created the maps from memory.

SETTLING DOWN

Upon his return, Jolliet applied for trading rights to the lands he had explored along the Illinois River, but his request was refused. He was, however, granted land on the lower Saint Lawrence River, where he began to farm. He explored the route from that river up the Saguenay and its tributaries to Lake Mistassini. In 1694 he explored and charted more than 300 miles of Labrador's coast. He died six years later.

On June 14, 1671, Jolliet, a handful of other Frenchmen, and members of fourteen different Native American groups gathered at Sault Sainte Marie to hear Daumont de Saint-Lusson declare,

In the name of . . . Louis, . . . Most Christian King of France . . . I take possession of this place . . . as also of Lakes Huron and Superior . . . and all countries, rivers, lakes, and streams contiguous and adjacent thereunto: both those which have been discovered and those which may be discovered hereafter.

Quoted in Francis Parkman, *The Discovery of the Great West* (1869)

1645
Louis Jolliet is born in Quebec.

1667
Spends a year in France.

1673
Leaves with Jacques Marquette on Mississippi expedition.

1675
Marries and settles on lower Saint Lawrence River.

1679
Explores Hudson Bay.

1694
Explores Labrador coast.

1700
Dies.

SEE ALSO

• Champlain, Samuel de

• La Salle, René-Robert Cavelier de

• Marquette, Jacques

KINO, EUSEBIO FRANCISCO

OF THE MANY MISSIONARIES who traveled from Europe to the New World to spread the Christian faith, Eusebio Francisco Kino (1645–1711) was one of the most remarkable. Sent to preach to the Pima people of present-day southern Arizona and northern Mexico, Kino also explored and mapped the region and brought some important technological innovations to the Pima. Although Kino was, in principle, a servant of the Spanish Empire, he strove to protect his congregations from exploitation by Spanish landlords and colonial officials.

Left **This statue of Kino portrays him as part missionary, part cowboy.**

THE SOCIETY OF JESUS

Born Eusebio Francisco Chino (also written Chini and Kühn) in the town of Segno in the mountainous Tirol region of Italy, Kino was educated at a Roman Catholic school. At the age of eighteen, he fell seriously ill and was close to death. Kino's family and close friends prayed to Saint Francis Xavier, joint founder of the Society of Jesus (also known as the Jesuits), a Roman Catholic order noted for its charitable, educational, and missionary work. When Kino made a full recovery, he vowed to become a Jesuit.

Between 1665 and 1681 Kino trained as a Jesuit missionary priest, first in Bavaria (in southern Germany) and later in Spain. It was

The Pima

The Pima called themselves the "river people" and lived along the Gila and Salt Rivers in present-day Arizona. They dwelled in well-organized, peaceful villages larger than those of their neighbors and lived on maize and vegetables grown and harvested communally. During regular droughts they hunted animals and gathered wild beans. They were friendly toward European settlers. Their native culture was soon dominated by the colonizers'.

Right In this drawing a Pima mother is attending to her young child outside a thatch-and-mud-covered lodge that is typical of Pima homes.

1645
Eusebio Kino is born in the Austrian-ruled Italian Tirol.

1663
Falls seriously ill but makes a full recovery.

1665
Begins training as a Jesuit missionary.

1678
Is chosen to go to New Spain (Mexico).

1681
Arrives at Veracruz, Mexico.

1685
Leads an unsuccessful mission to Lower California.

1687
Moves to the Pimeria Alta and establishes a mission at Nuestra Señora de los Dolores.

1700–1702
Travels the Colorado River and proves that California is not an island.

during this time that his skills as a mathematician emerged, skills that were to prove extremely useful to him in later years when he began to draw maps of the American Southwest.

At the age of thirty-six, Kino arrived in the Spanish colony of New Spain (present-day Mexico), and four years later he was sent on an expedition whose purpose was to colonize Lower California (an area in present-day northwestern Mexico). When severe drought led to the mission being aborted, Kino was ordered to begin work to the east of Lower California, in the isolated Pimeria Alta region of the Sonora Desert (in present-day Arizona).

PASTOR AND EXPLORER

In 1687 Kino established a mission at Nuestra Señora de los Dolores. After four years, with his mission base secure, Kino made the first of some forty-five journeys—on which he was often the only European—to explore the arid region and to meet (and convert) the native peoples.

Kino produced the first detailed maps of the areas he covered in his journeys, which included long stretches of three rivers: the Colorado, the Rio Grande, and the Gila. Two of his longest and most celebrated expeditions took place between 1700 and 1702, when he traveled down the Colorado to the Gulf of California and so proved that California was not an island. It is estimated that, in all, Kino traveled some 8,000 miles (12,000 km) across 50,000 square miles (almost 13 million hectares) of trackless desert.

1703
Kino's map of Baja California is published in Munich, Germany.

1705
Historical Memoir of Pimeria Alta is published.

1711
Kino dies.

HELPING COMMUNITIES TO DEVELOP

To the peoples he encountered, Kino brought not only Christianity but also, in many cases, opportunities for increased prosperity. He introduced sheep, horses, cattle ranching, and wheat growing and in this way helped to bring many Native Americans greater wealth and economic stability. He established nineteen cattle-breeding ranches, one of many measures that helped native peoples to survive the periodic droughts that had plagued the region for centuries.

Kino further helped the Pima, a people native to present-day Arizona, by providing them with new technological skills; they learned how to build better roads and how to work wood and metal. He also helped the Pima resist the attacks of their hostile neighbors, the Apache. Perhaps most significantly, he insisted on upholding a royal decree, often ignored, that native peoples who accepted Christianity were exempt from paying tribute and from laboring in the mines.

HISTORICAL MEMOIR

Kino remained in the Pimeria Alta for the remainder of his life and died at midnight on March 15, 1711, in Magdalena Sonora, Mexico, where he had come to dedicate a new chapel to Saint Francis Xavier, his patron saint. Kino's remains were buried beneath the chapel floor.

Kino is remembered as a compassionate man and a practical priest who could say mass, map a river, and round up cattle with equal facility. His maps were used long after his death, and his *Historical Memoir of Pimeria Alta*, a record of his life and of his many explorations published in 1705, remains an invaluable source for historians and anthropologists.

SEE ALSO

• Spain

LAND TRANSPORT

FOR TENS OF THOUSANDS OF YEARS, the earliest explorers traveled on foot. When people learned to train beasts of burden (horses and camels, for example) to pull wheeled vehicles, they were able to carry more food and water, as well as goods to trade with strangers, and thus could travel farther from centers of civilization. With the invention of the internal combustion engine in the late nineteenth century, explorers had at their disposal new forms of transport that would open up entire continents. By the middle of the twentieth century, motor vehicles were widely used in journeys of exploration. In the late twentieth century, electrically powered land vehicles were used to explore the surface of other planets.

Below **The horse, reintroduced to the Americas by European settlers in the sixteenth century, was used by Native Americans to pull a travois, a wheelless carriage that provided a bumpy ride.**

60,000–4,500 BCE
Traveling on foot, humans colonize habitable areas of the earth.

C. 5000 BCE
Cattle are first used for transport.

C. 3500 BCE
The wheel is used for the first time in land transport.

C. 2000 BCE
Horses are used to pull vehicles.

C. 500–200 BCE
Gradual emergence of the Silk Road between China and Europe encourages both trade and exploration.

1509 CE
Hernán Cortés brings first horses to mainland America: eleven stallions, five mares, and a foal arrive in Mexico.

1885
Internal combustion engine revolutionizes land transport.

EARLY 1900s
Polar explorers use teams of dogs and sleds to reach the North and South Poles.

Left **This clay model of an early wheeled vehicle pulled by two mules was found in the Indus valley city of Mohenjo Daro and dates from around 2500 BCE.**

PREHISTORIC MIGRATION

Starting out from Africa around 60,000 years ago, humans ventured throughout the world on foot in search of new land to settle. Small groups first settled in western Asia and Europe and later spread eastward across the vast Eurasian landmass. As they walked, they probably hauled essential belongings behind them on simple racks of branches and twine. By around 12,000 years ago, humans had spread as far as the eastern tip of Russia. At that time Asia and North America were joined by a land bridge; crossing this bridge over a relatively short period of time, which archaeologists estimate to be around two thousand years, people colonized both North and South America. Four thousand years ago the Inuit moved north toward the Arctic and settled the far north of Canada and, eventually, Greenland, among the earth's bleakest and least hospitable areas.

1957–1958
First crossing of the Antarctic using motor vehicles is made.

1970
Radio-controlled vehicle *Lunokhod 1* lands on the moon.

1971–1972
Lunar Rover transports American astronauts around the moon.

1997
Radio-controlled vehicle *Sojourner* lands on Mars.

The Wheel

*T*he invention of the wheel, the most important development in the history of land transport, is dated to the fourth millennium BCE. The earliest known wheeled vehicles were used by the ancient civilization centered around Sumer (in present-day southern Iraq) and are thought to have developed from the potter's wheel, use of which is recorded in Egypt around 3500 BCE. The first wheeled vehicles were wooden carts with four wheels. Sumerian picture writing and early clay models of such vehicles suggest that they were pulled by beasts of burden, such as oxen. Not until 2000 BCE were horses harnessed to carts and, later, to chariots.

Ancient peoples, especially those that flourished in the area of western Asia known as the Fertile Crescent (which extends around the southeastern coast of the Mediterranean), used wheeled vehicles to aid their exploration of the lands that surrounded them and to strengthen their armies in warfare. Alexander the Great (356–323 BCE), for example, conquered a huge area of land that stretched from the Mediterranean to northern India. He would not have enjoyed his remarkable military successes without the animal transport he used to supply his army and the cavalry and horse-drawn chariots he deployed so effectively in battle.

Above **This grouping of silver figurines includes an Incan woman with an alpaca (left) and a llama (center), two sturdy animals that were for thousands of years the main method of transport for the native peoples of South America.**

EARLY ANIMAL TRANSPORT

Around 10,000 BCE, when an increasing portion of the world's habitable regions were being settled, people began to develop the first farms, settlements on which crops were cultivated and animals were reared. As they became more skilled at farming, people also began to use animals as means of transport. The use of oxen to carry people and produce may date back to about 5000 BCE, and the use of horses to around 2000 BCE.

Although horses were the most commonly used and effective means of land transport, in the desert regions of northern Africa and Asia, in addition to horses, camels proved effective pack animals and coped better with the arid environment. In South America the llama performed a similar role, and in the mountainous regions of central Asia, local inhabitants preferred the yak. Not until the invention of the steam-powered locomotive and the internal combustion engine in the nineteenth century were these animals superseded by faster and more efficient forms of transport.

THE SILK ROAD

Throughout history one of the principal motives for exploration was the desire of one people to find other peoples with whom to trade goods. Some of the most important land routes between continents were trade routes. The most famous ancient trade route was the Silk Road, used regularly from the first century BCE as a means of transporting silk, spices, gold, and other luxuries from China to the Roman Empire and metals, jewels, horses, and even pistachio nuts the other way.

Transport along the Silk Road was generally by a caravan of camels across the deserts and, where available, yaks across the mountainous stretches. The journey from one end of the Silk Road to the other took on average three years, and the risks, from natural hazards and also from bandits, were high. The Silk Road passed through all extremes of temperature, from scorching deserts to freezing snowbound mountain passes. One desert on the route was named the Takla Makan, which roughly translates, "You go in, but you do not come out."

Below **The cave paintings at Lascaux, France, date from around 15,000 BCE and include the earliest known human depictions of horses.**

The History of the Horse

Since prehistoric times the horse has been one of the most effective methods of land transport. The species familiar in the modern world, called *Equus*, came originally from North America, from where it spread southward to South America and west, over the Alaskan land bridge, to Asia, Europe, and Africa. By the end of the last Ice Age (around 10,000 BCE) horses were common in Europe, and they feature in cave paintings of this period, such as those at Lascaux in France. The earliest evidence of the human use of horses—by people living on the steppes (grassy plains) of central Asia—is provided by clay tablets that date from around 2000 BCE.

When the first European explorers visited America in the sixteenth century, they took horses with them. As *Equus* had died out in its native land long before, the peoples the Europeans encountered were spellbound and terrified by the animals and their human riders. The Spanish conquistador Francisco Pizarro owed his extraordinary conquest of the Incas and subsequent settlement of Peru to his cavalry troops. With the advantage of maneuverability, speed, and height, in 1532 at Cajamarca a small force of 177 men, which included 67 mounted soldiers, was able to defeat an Inca army of perhaps 40,000. By the middle of the seventeenth century, Native American peoples, such as the Apache, were using horses for transport and warfare.

Africa, the Americas, and Australia

During the nineteenth century, many of the world's explorers focused their attention on the uncharted interiors of Africa, the Americas, and Australia, venturing into the unknown on foot, horse, or camel or by canoe.

Railroads

By the mid-nineteenth century much of the American continent had been explored and mapped and the building of railroads began on both the east and west coasts of the United States. A significant milestone was reached when, on May 10, 1869, the eastern Union Pacific Railroad and the western Central Pacific Railroad joined up near the town of Promontory, Utah. The driving of the final rivet linking the rails from east and west was reported by telegraph, which ran alongside the rails, and was celebrated in every city in the United States.

The railroad opened up the western North American continent and enabled settlers to arrive in great numbers in much greater comfort and speed than was provided by the previous method of transport—the horse- or ox-drawn wagon. The transcontinental railroad network was so successful that in 1887 the U.S. government was forced to introduce legislation restricting the profits that could be made from rail fares for both passengers and goods.

Right **This official photograph shows a ceremony marking the completion of the Denver and Rio Grande Railroad in 1885—one of many railroads built across the United States during the second half of the nineteenth century.**

THE POLES

By the end of the nineteenth century, much of the surface of the world had been explored. At the start of the twentieth century, several adventurers joined the race to be the first to reach the North and South Poles. The ones who succeeded, Peary (probably the first explorer to reach the North Pole), and Amundsen (the first to reach the South Pole), did so by copying the Inuit peoples of the Arctic in using husky dogs and sleds. Those who failed, Scott and Shackleton, favored the use of ponies or "manhauling" (having people pull sleds).

Scott took three motor sleds on his doomed 1911 attempt to reach the South Pole. One fell through the ice as soon as it was hauled off his ship, and the other two quickly broke down. It was only between the First and Second World Wars that motor vehicles became of any real use to polar explorers. In 1957 and 1958 the British-led Trans-Antarctic Expedition undertook the first successful overland crossing of the Antarctic using lightweight tracked vehicles. The SnoCats and Ferguson tractors proved to be a great success over flat land, where they were able to move quickly and pull heavy loads, but ran into difficulties during attempts to cross crevasses. The Ferguson tractors had a boxlike canvas cover to offer the driver some protection from the cold. The SnoCats, in comparison, were quite luxurious. The vehicles were painted bright orange to stand out clearly against the snow. Some modern explorers at the Poles make use of wind power, using parachute-like sails and skis to scoot across the ice.

Animals and Polar Transport

*T*eams of dogs, usually huskies bred within the Arctic Circle, are ideally suited to polar exploration. They cope well with the long sea journey to either Pole and eat meat from animals that can be hunted and killed during the journey—seals, penguins, polar bears, and even, if it becomes necessary, each other. Other animals that were used in early polar exploration, such as Manchurian ponies, did not cope well with the extreme polar temperatures. Their herbivorous diet was also a problem. Both polar regions are devoid of vegetation, and great supplies of hay and other fodder had to be transported with the ponies.

Left **During the 1957–1958 Trans-Antarctic Expedition, disaster was averted when this SnoCat motor vehicle narrowly avoided plummeting into a crevasse; it was towed out of danger by other motor vehicles.**

Above The *Lunar Rover* was transported to the moon in 1972 aboard *Apollo 17*.

Mountains

Once the Poles had been conquered, remote mountain ranges such as the Himalayas were among the last places on earth yet to be explored. Four-wheel-drive vehicles and tough army trucks can penetrate only so far, and many mountainous areas are inaccessible to motorized land transport. As a result, twenty-first century mountaineers who wish to explore the Himalayas overland have to resort to the method used by travelers of the Silk Road two thousand years ago: the yak.

SEE ALSO

• Caravan • Polar Exploration • Silk Road

• Space Exploration • Trade

Extraterrestrial Transport

Advances in motor-vehicle technology have had an important influence on extraterrestrial land vehicles (used in the exploration of the moon and of other planets). In 1970, the Soviet Union landed an unmanned radio-controlled vehicle called *Lunokhod 1* on the moon. Between 1971 and 1972 American astronauts took an electric vehicle called the *Lunar Rover* to the moon. This spindly vehicle was made as lightweight as possible to restrict the load the launch rocket would have to carry beyond the gravitational pull of earth. The seats, for example, were made of strips of canvas. The rover was slightly over ten feet long and six feet wide and could carry two passengers at eight miles an hour. It had a radio antenna shaped like an umbrella for communicating with earth and with the lunar landing module. There was also a television camera mounted at the front of the vehicle. The *Lunar Rover* enabled astronauts to make journeys of exploration across the surface of the moon.

In 1997 a remote-controlled land vehicle called *Sojourner* was used to examine the surface of Mars. Around the size of a microwave oven and powered by solar panels that harnessed energy from the sun, it trundled about, analyzing rock and soil samples.

La Salle, René-Robert Cavelier de

BORN IN FRANCE IN 1643, the French explorer René-Robert Cavelier de La Salle discovered the mouth of the Mississippi River and claimed the entire valley of that river for France. His dream of establishing a strong French presence on the Mississippi failed, however, when a colonizing expedition ended in disaster and, in 1687, in his own death.

Rebellious Youth

René-Robert Cavelier de La Salle was born into an aristocratic family, and as a young man, at his father's request, he began training to join the Jesuits (a Roman Catholic order noted for its missionary work). However, the spirited René-Robert did not fit well into the disciplined Jesuit mold. When he was twenty-two, his father died, and soon afterward he left the Jesuits.

According to French law, La Salle had given up all claims to his father's estate when he began his Jesuit training. Although he was left with little material wealth, he had great ambitions that he hoped would one day lead to glory for France—and for himself.

La Salle's Character

La Salle often suspected that others were plotting against him. He once wrote, "I know of no friends in [France].... I open my mind to nobody, I distrust everybody." He had enormous energy, a fiery temper, and few friends, one exception being Henri de Tonty (1650–1704), a soldier who had lost a hand fighting for France.

To New France

In 1666 La Salle's hunger for adventure took him to Montreal, where Native Americans told him of a great river that ran to the west. La Salle believed the river might flow to China. If his hunch had proved correct, he would have found a water passage across the American continent—the goal of many early North American explorers.

Below **This romanticized view shows La Salle gazing at a map that displays Louisiana, the vast region of North America he claimed for King Louis XIV.**

In 1669 La Salle joined an expedition led by François Dollier and René de Galinée to explore the lands west of Montreal. The men traveled along the southern shore of Lake Ontario and heard the roar from nearby Niagara Falls but did not visit the site. While the rest of the party continued northwest, La Salle split off. Later claims that La Salle reached the Ohio River and followed it as far as present-day Louisville, Kentucky, have since proved false.

First Journeys and Trials

In 1673 La Salle met Louis de Buade, Count of Frontenac, the governor of New France. The two shared the dream of extending the French hold in North America and of gaining wealth from the areas around the Great Lakes. They also hoped to gain glory in the process.

La Salle made two trips back to France in the next few years. In the second, in 1677, he won the right to a monopoly on the trade in buffalo skins along the Mississippi. When he returned to New France in 1678, he and Frontenac illegally expanded this monopoly to cover trade in furs. They hoped that the profits would finance their pursuit of glory. La Salle sent traders into the Great Lakes to collect furs. He also had his friend Henri de Tonty oversee the building of a forty-five-ton ship on the Niagara River, near Lake Erie. La Salle intended to use this ship, the *Griffon*, to hold the vast store of furs his agents were

Right **This illustration, from Father Louis Hennepin's 1697 *New Discovery*, is the first printed image of Niagara Falls, which Hennepin said were six hundred feet (183 m) high—about three times their actual height.**

1643
La Salle is born in Rouen, France.

1666
Moves to New France.

1669
Joins the expedition of Dollier and Galinée as far as Niagara.

1673
Meets Louis de Buade, Count of Frontenac.

1677
Receives permission from king of France to explore Mississippi River valley.

1679
Builds the *Griffon* on Lake Erie.

1682
Explores the Mississippi River to its mouth.

1684
Sets off from France to colonize the mouth of the Mississippi; lands in Texas.

1687
Is killed by his men while heading for his fort on the Ilinois River.

expected to collect and to impress Native Americans with the power of France.

The *Griffon* was finished in the summer of 1679, and La Salle set sail. He made several stops to collect furs from his agents. Yet there was bad news. La Salle learned that a ship carrying supplies from France had sunk and that some of his followers had deserted. He also had pressing debts back in Montreal.

La Salle ordered the furs to be sent to Montreal, where they could be sold and the proceeds used to settle his debts. The *Griffon* was never heard from again; it may have sunk in a storm but was more likely sunk by rival traders with the help of Ottawa Indians. Unaware of this disaster, La Salle pressed on.

Father Louis Hennepin *1626–1701*

*B*orn in present-day Belgium, Louis Hennepin became a friar with the Recollect order (a branch of the Franciscans) and, at the age of forty-nine, was sent to New France. In 1680 he joined La Salle, whose goal was to head down the Mississippi River. Hennepin and a few others were sent ahead as an advance party. Hennepin claimed that they canoed to the river's mouth and back. Since doing so would have meant traveling more than three thousand miles by canoe in about six weeks, his claim is widely rejected. Hennepin and the others were captured by a band of Sioux and taken to the Mille Lacs area of present-day Minnesota. They regained their freedom five months after capture, and two years later Hennepin returned to France, where he recounted his exploits in *New Discovery of a Vast Country in America*.

Left La Salle's *Griffon*, pictured here on Lake Erie, was the first sailing ship built for commerce on the Great Lakes. According to Louis Hennepin (who stands on the quarterdeck), Native Americans thought of it as a traveling fort.

Claiming Louisiana

As determined as ever to conquer new territory, La Salle moved down the Illinois River and made peace with the Native Americans there. He built a fort (Crévecoeur) near the river, where he left Tonty, and went back to New France to settle his debts and obtain more supplies. During the following year, he trekked back to New France, ordered his affairs, and returned to the Illinois to find Tonty missing and the fort burned during an attack by Iroquois. La Salle finally reunited with Tonty, and in February 1682 the men set off down the Mississippi. By April they had reached the Gulf of Mexico. La Salle grandly "took possession of that river, of all rivers that

enter it and of all the country watered by them" in the name of the king of France.

La Salle's End

On returning to New France, La Salle found that Frontenac, his ally, had been replaced. He dismissed this new setback and sailed back to France to promote his new plan—to plant a colony at the mouth of the Mississippi. On the basis of La Salle's promises of the riches that could be obtained for France, especially if Spanish silver mines in Mexico were raided, the king agreed. He named La Salle the viceroy of the region from the Illinois River to the Mississippi's mouth. On July 24, 1684, La Salle sailed from France with a small fleet and a company of settlers.

Unfortunately, the ships overshot their goal by about 400 miles and in February 1685 landed at Matagorda Bay in Texas. La Salle built a fort, but the stay in Texas was disastrous. Two ships were wrecked, and their supplies were destroyed. The largest sailed back to France after its captain quarreled with La Salle. The survivors now had no way out but overland. Meanwhile, many settlers were falling ill and dying.

La Salle tried several times to find the Mississippi and to unite with Tonty, who was coming down the river to join his leader. As the months passed, La Salle's small colony dwindled from nearly two hundred people to fewer than fifty, and the situation became desperate. In January 1687 La Salle set out with a small group to try to reach his fort on the Illinois. On March 19 some of his men mutinied and killed him. A few of the party did continue, reaching a fort that Tonty had built along the Arkansas River, near the Mississippi. They returned to France and told the sad tale of the explorer's death. Meanwhile, of the few survivors in Texas, some were killed in an attack by Native Americans, and others fell into Spanish hands.

Below **In 1682 La Salle claimed the Mississippi River and its valley for France, naming the area Louisiana after King Louis XIV.**

Pyle.

A New Discovery of a Large Country in AMERICA by Father Lewis Hennepin

A
New Discovery
OF A
Vaſt Country in AMERICA,
Extending above Four Thouſand Miles,
BETWEEN
New France and New Mexico;
WITH A
Deſcription of the Great Lakes, Cataraſts, Rivers, Plants, and Animals.

Alſo, the Manners, Cuſtoms, and Languages of the ſeveral Native Indians; and the Advantage of Commerce with thoſe different Nations.

WITH A
CONTINUATION,
Giving an ACCOUNT of the
Attempts of the Sieur De la SALLE upon the
Mines of St. Barbe, &c. The Taking of
Quebec by the Engliſh; With the Advantages
of a Shorter Cut to China and Japan.

Both Parts Illuſtrated with Maps, and Figures, and Dedicated to His Majeſty K. William.

By L. Hennepin, now Reſident in Holland.

To which are added, Several New Diſcoveries in North-America, not publiſh'd in the French Edition.

LONDON, Printed for M. Bentley, J. Tonſon, H. Bonwick, T. Goodwin, and S. Manſkip. 1698.

La Salle's trusted second-in-command, Henri de Tonty, left an account of their journey down the Mississippi River in 1682:

We proceeded on our course, and after going forty leagues, arrived at the sea on the 7th of April. [Monsieur] de La Salle sent canoes to inspect the channels. Some went to the channel on the right hand, some to the left, and [Monsieur] de La Salle chose that in the center. In the evening each made his report, that is to say, that the channels were very fine, wide, and deep. We encamped on the right bank, erected the arms of the King, and returned several times to inspect the channels.

Henri de Tonty, *Memoirs*

Above **Father Louis Hennepin's *New Discovery*, first published in France in 1697, became an extremely popular book in Europe. It is now known, however, that not all of the facts or adventures recounted in it are accurate.**

SEE ALSO

• Champlain, Samuel de • Jolliet, Louis
• Marquette, Jacques

LATITUDE AND LONGITUDE

EVERY SPOT ON EARTH CAN BE PINPOINTED to within around one hundred feet (30 m) by a system of map referencing that places an object at the intersection of a line of latitude and a line of longitude. (Lines of latitude circle the earth from east to west; lines of longitude run north and south.) For example, a person standing at 40°45'00" north and 73°52'30" west is in the middle of Central Park, New York City. The system is an essential aid to navigation, especially for sailors at sea or pilots flying over the sea, where there are no landmarks. In addition, the system, whose first use is recorded around 300 BCE, is an important component of twenty-first century Global Positioning System (GPS) technology.

Below **This French map shows the world as envisaged by the ancient Greek astronomer and geographer Ptolemy, who was one of the first mapmakers to include lines of latitude and longitude.**

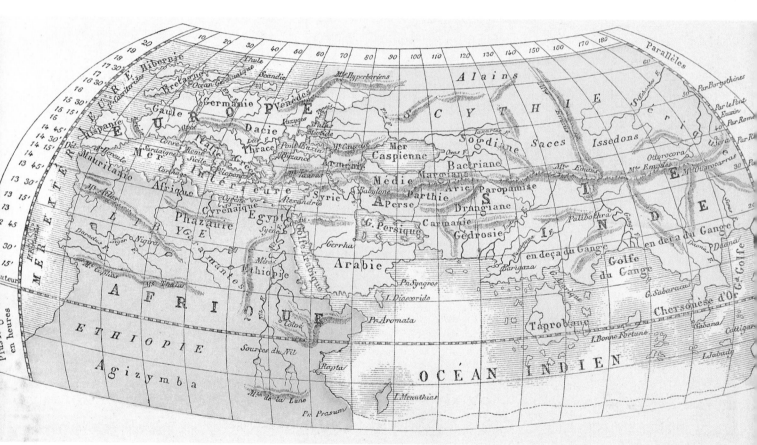

c. 245 BCE
Eratosthenes of Cyrene is the first mapmaker to use a grid reference system.

1410 CE
With the republication of Ptolemy's *Geography* in Bologna, Italy, the first printed maps to show latitude and longitude become available in Europe.

1598
Philip II of Spain offers the first prize for the discovery of a means of measuring longitude at sea.

1675
Greenwich Observatory is founded by Charles II.

1714
British government offers a £20,000 longitude prize.

1759
John Harrison produces the first accurate pocket-sized chronometer.

1884
Greenwich Observatory becomes site of the prime meridian.

1990s
GPS (Global Positioning System) becomes generally available.

LATITUDE

A measurement of latitude indicates a position north or south of the equator, the circle around the world midway between the North and South Poles. Lines of latitude are called parallels because they circle the globe parallel to the equator. Latitude is measured in degrees (°). The equator is zero degrees (0°), the North Pole is 90° north, and the South Pole is 90° south. The tropics of Cancer and Capricorn are both parallels; their latitudes are 23.5° north and 23.5° south, respectively. Lines of latitude are somewhat closer together at the poles, and so the length of a degree of latitude varies. On average, each degree is around sixty-nine miles (111 km).

LONGITUDE

A measurement of longitude indicates a position east or west of the Greenwich meridian, an imaginary line that runs north and south through Greenwich, London. All lines of longitude, known as meridians, run from the North to the South Pole and divide the globe into segments, much like those of an orange. Like latitude, longitude is measured in degrees. The Greenwich meridian is 0°, and meridians are spaced out to a maximum of 180° east or

The International Date Line

When it is noon in Greenwich, it is midnight along the international date line, which runs through the Bering Straits between Alaska and the eastern tip of Russia and down through the Pacific. The international date line almost follows the 180° meridian, erring from east or west into open ocean to avoid any one spot where it can be both today and tomorrow on the same island or country.

west of Greenwich. The length of a degree of longitude varies from sixty-nine miles (111 km) at the equator, to zero miles at the Poles, where all meridians converge.

MINUTES AND SECONDS

Each degree of latitude and longitude is further divided into sixty sections called minutes. Each minute of latitude and longitude may in turn be further divided into sixty sections called seconds. Minutes are written ' and seconds are written ". Therefore, the reference for Central Park of 40°45'00"N and 73°52'30"W means a latitude reading of 40 degrees, 45 minutes, and 0 seconds north of the equator and a longitude reading of 73 degrees, 52 minutes, and 30 seconds west of Greenwich.

Left **This dashboard-mounted GPS device indicates the position of the car on an electronic map and can be used to suggest the best route for the driver to take.**

Above **Built in 1675, the Royal Observatory in Greenwich, south-eastern London, was designed by Sir Christopher Wren, the celebrated architect who also designed Saint Paul's Cathedral.**

MAP PIONEERS

The concept of latitude and longitude has been in existence since at least 300 BCE. The Greek geographer Eratosthenes of Cyrene (c. 276–c. 194 BCE) divided his map of the known world into parallels of latitude, which were equally spaced, and meridians of longitude, which were not. The Greek concept of latitude and longitude was transmitted to Europe through the work of Claudius Ptolemy (c. 90–168 CE), whose *Geography* was first published in Italy in 1410.

THE SEARCH FOR A PRIME MERIDIAN

Once the concept of a round rather than flat world became generally accepted, the world's mapmakers quickly agreed on a central reference point for latitude—the equator was an obvious choice as a 0° parallel. However, it took a lot longer to establish a 0° meridian (a prime meridian)—after all, any one line of longitude could be used to divide east from west. Eratosthenes and Ptolemy chose Alexandria, Egypt, as the prime meridian for their maps. During the Middle Ages, Arab geographers selected a point 10° east of Baghdad, and many Europeans used the Canary Islands and later the Cape Verde Islands. During the Age of Exploration, the great seafaring powers (Spain, Portugal, England, and the Netherlands) used lines of longitude running through their own nation. As national mapping programs were launched in the late eighteenth century, this trend continued. Paris (France), Boston, Philadelphia, and Washington, DC (United States), Rome (Italy), and Saint Petersburg (Russia) all appeared on maps as the prime meridian. Maps were not standardized until the late nineteenth century.

The location of a standard prime meridian was eventually resolved in 1884, when, despite some reluctance from certain other nations, the British persuaded the world to accept the Greenwich Observatory in London as the site. At the time Britain ruled the world's largest empire and had the world's most powerful navy. Furthermore, a British geographer (John Harrison) had done more than anyone else to solve the problem of determining longitude at sea. For these reasons and others, it seemed appropriate to settle on the Greenwich Observatory as the starting point.

The Royal Greenwich Observatory

Founded in 1675 by King Charles II, the Greenwich Observatory was set up on a hill overlooking the Thames River to the southeast of London. First and foremost, the observatory's intended role was to find a way of establishing the longitude of British ships at sea. Scientists made minutely detailed records of the positions of the moon, sun, stars, and planets at specific times of the year and compiled charts for use by navigators. In 1884 the observatory was chosen as the location of the prime meridian, which is still marked by an iron bar set in the ground. Visitors to the observatory can stand with one foot in the Eastern Hemisphere and one in the Western. Work carried out at the observatory made a major contribution to navigational records and in more recent times also led to the discovery of satellites (moons) of the planets Jupiter, Neptune, and Uranus.

When it was first built, the observatory was some way out of London. By the beginning of the twentieth century, however, London had expanded to such an extent that Greenwich was no longer a rural district but rather part of the urban sprawl. As the haze of smoke and light created by the city made astronomical observation increasingly difficult, the astronomical research of the observatory was relocated first to East Sussex in southern England from 1957 and finally to Cambridge from 1990. As a cost-cutting measure, the Astronomy Research Council shut down the observatory in 1998 and moved its equipment and operations to Edinburgh, Scotland.

Left The dividing line between the Eastern and Western Hemispheres is marked at Greenwich by an iron bar set in the ground.

Working out One's Location

Ancient and medieval navigators calculated their position at sea with an astrolabe, whose use involved much guesswork. In 1731 came the invention of the sextant, an essential seafarer's tool whose measurement of the height of the sun or of a particular star above the horizon was much more precise than that of an astrolabe.

In theory longitude should be as easy to calculate: for every 15° traveled east, local time moves forward an hour, and for every 15° traveled west, time moves backward an hour. For example, if it is noon at Greenwich (0°), it is 1:00 PM in Vienna, Austria (16°E), and 11:00 AM in Dakar, Senegal (17°W). To determine longitude, therefore, a seafarer needed to note when the sun reached its highest point in the sky (that is, noon) and then to consult a clock set to Greenwich time. For example, a point where it is noon at the same time that it is three o'clock in Greenwich would have a longitude of 45° west.

Clocks at Sea

Before the invention of radio transmission and satellite communication, it was not easy for a navigator at sea to know what time it was in Greenwich. Until the eighteenth century, sea clocks were extremely inaccurate.

Right **The sextant was one of the seafarer's most essential tools. This engraving was taken from a 1797 edition of the** *Encyclopaedia Britannica.*

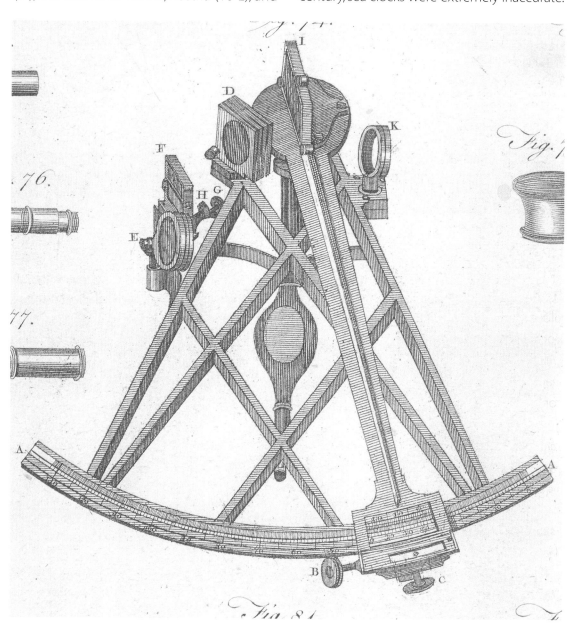

Clock mechanisms were based either on springs or on a pendulum and were easily disrupted by the motion of the waves and by the extremes of hot and cold and of dryness and moisture that prevail aboard a ship. The key to establishing a sound measurement of longitude lay in developing a clock that could keep accurate time at sea.

The impossibility of establishing longitude caused navigators considerable problems. In 1707 a major disaster in the British navy—four warships ran into rocks off the Scilly Isles (off the southwestern coast of England) and two thousand men drowned—finally spurred the British government into action. A Board of Longitude was established to come up with a solution, and a prize of £20,000 (then a vast sum) was offered to anyone who could solve the problem of determining longitude at sea. Essentially, the challenge was to invent a clock that would remain accurate during a sea voyage. The prizewinner was an English clock maker named John Harrison (1693–1776), whose exceptionally accurate chronometer, H4, was completed in 1759.

GPS

By the year 2000, a series of twenty-four satellites orbiting the earth were operating the Global Positioning System (GPS), whereby a pocket-sized instrument, by communicating with the satellites, could give an instant reading of latitude and longitude. Millennia of conjecture had come to an end.

Right **John Flamsteed was the first "astronomer royal," the grand title given to the chief scientist of the Greenwich Observatory.**

SEE ALSO

- Astronomical Instruments • Chronometer
- Global Positioning System • Mapmaking
- Map Projection • Navigation
- Navigational Instruments

John Flamsteed *1646–1719*

*T*he first man to hold the position of astronomer royal, the chief astronomer at the Greenwich Observatory, was John Flamsteed. In 1676 Flamsteed began work on updating and correcting previous astronomical tables, to which task he brought a new standard of accuracy. His lifelong devotion to his job resulted in the publication, six years after his death, of *Historia Coelestis Britannica*, which lists the position of over three thousand fixed stars. This remarkably detailed work was an invaluable aid to seafarers, who could use the information it contained to calculate their latitude and longitude at sea.

Flamsteed's observations of the moon also provided astronomical information that was essential for the British physicist Sir Isaac Newton to prove his theory of gravity.

FLAMSTEED.

LA VÉRENDRYE, PIERRE GAULTIER DE VARENNES DE

THE CANADIAN-BORN EXPLORER Pierre Gaultier de Varennes de La Vérendrye (1685–1749) dreamed of finding the Sea of the West, a fabled body of water connected to the North American river system that would provide a passage across the continent to the Pacific Ocean. Although La Vérendrye failed to find any such passage, by setting up fur trading posts between Lake Superior and the lakes of Manitoba, he and his sons opened up western Canada for future exploration.

Left **La Vérendrye is depicted here at Fort Saint-Charles, which he established at Lake of the Woods in 1732.**

EARLY YEARS

Pierre Gaultier de Varennes was born the youngest of thirteen children in Trois-Rivières, Quebec, on November 17, 1685. During the previous hundred years, the area had been colonized by French settlers and given the name New France. Most of the settlers were farmers; others engaged in fur trading and fishing, but it was a tough and unpredictable way of life. From an early age Pierre dreamed that one day he would press farther into the unexplored wilderness of North America to make his own fortune.

ARMY LIFE

When he was twelve, Pierre joined the colonial troops. By the time he was twenty, he was fighting the English in New England and

---

NOVEMBER 17, 1685
La Vérendrye is born in Trois-Rivières, Canada.

1704–1705
Fights against the English in New England and Newfoundland.

1707–1712
Fights for the French in the War of the Spanish Succession.

1712
Marries Marie-Anne Dandonneau du Sablé and settles in Trois-Rivières.

1726
Joins his brother's fur-trading business near Lake Superior.

JUNE 8, 1731
Sets out from Montreal on first expedition to find the Sea of the West.

1731
Builds Fort Saint-Pierre on Rainy Lake.

1732
Builds Fort Saint-Charles on Lake of the Woods.

1733
Builds a trading post on the Red River.

1734
Fort Maurepas is constructed at Lake Winnipeg; La Vérendrye returns to Montreal.

1735
Sets out on second expedition.

The Fur Traders

*F*rench fur traders were forced to venture ever farther into unexplored regions of Canada as demand for fur increased, especially after 1670, when the English began to set up competing trading posts along the shore of Hudson Bay. As the traders penetrated westward, they set up fortified trading posts to protect their interests from rivals. Some explorers, such as La Vérendrye, were given licenses to trade in furs in order to cover the costs of exploration. When La Vérendrye spent more effort trading than exploring, he was harshly criticized. Even the Canadian governor Charles de Beauharnois, who supported La Vérendrye, claimed that French explorers "were after beaver, not the Sea of the West."

Left **In this engraving Native Americans trade fur for guns at a busy trading post in Manitoba.**

Newfoundland. In 1707 he went to France to fight in the War of the Spanish Succession, in which France, Spain, and Bavaria defended the right of Philip of Bourbon to ascend the Spanish throne. La Vérendrye was made a lieutenant and braved injury and imprisonment before his return to New France in 1712. When his oldest brother, Louis, was killed in action, Pierre inherited the family title, La Vérendrye.

1736
La Vérendrye's son Jean-Baptiste is killed by Sioux at Lake of the Woods.

1738
La Vérendrye reaches the mouth of the Assiniboine River and builds Fort La Reine. Fort Rouge is built where Winnipeg is now located. La Vérendrye reaches North Dakota.

1742
La Vérendrye's son Pierre establishes Fort Dauphin on Lake Dauphin and Fort Bourbon on Cedar Lake.

1743
La Vérendrye's other sons Louis-Joseph and François travel west and perhaps reach the Big Horn Mountains.

1744
La Vérendrye returns with his sons to Montreal.

DECEMBER 5, 1749
Dies in Montreal.

Family Man

La Vérendrye returned to Trois-Rivières and, in the fall of 1712, married his childhood sweetheart, Marie-Anne Dandonneau du Sablé, with whom he had four boys and two girls. For many years he supported his family by farming, but he never abandoned his dream of becoming an explorer. In 1726 he took up his brother Jacques-René's offer of a post in his fur trading business near Lake Superior.

Search for the Sea of the West

While he was working with his brother, La Vérendrye became fascinated by stories he heard, from Native American traders visiting the post, of a great Sea of the West. He reasoned that such a sea would connect the American river system to the Pacific Ocean and thus would lead him to Asia. La Vérendrye was inspired to search for the Sea of the West and realized that a fur trade monopoly was the only way in which he could make enough money to pay for an expedition. He approached the governor of the French colony, Charles de Beauharnois, and requested a fur trade monopoly. Beauharnois gave La Vérendrye permission to travel westward and set up fur trading forts along his route to finance his exploration.

Exploring the Western Prairies

La Vérendrye set off from Montreal with his sons and nephew in June 1731. Having passed through Fort Kaministikwia (present-day Thunder Bay) on the western shore of Lake Superior, the men established Fort Saint-Pierre on Rainy Lake, where they tasted their first bitterly cold winter and were forced to stay put until spring. The following year La Vérendrye and his sons set up Fort Saint-Charles on Lake of the Woods, and in 1733 they reached the Red River. In 1734 La Vérendrye returned to Montreal, having covered nearly 2,500 miles (4,000 km).

Fur Trappers' Canoes

Explorers survived in the Canadian wilderness by using skills they learned from Native American fur trappers. La Vérendrye used large birch-bark canoes developed by the French from the much smaller native canoes. The canoe was made by using pine roots to sew pieces of bark onto an ash-wood frame. The canoe was then made watertight with a boiled mixture of pine gum and grease. Even the largest of these canoes, some of which were up to forty feet (12 m) long, were light enough to be carried by a few men overland between lakes and rivers.

THE DANGEROUS WEST

In 1735 La Vérendrye left Montreal once again and returned to the west. On his first western expedition La Vérendrye had traded with Native Americans, especially the Assiniboine and Cree, and they had seemed to pose no threat. Unfortunately, by allying himself with these peoples and trading guns with them, La Vérendrye had made an enemy of their traditional foes, the Dakota Sioux. In the summer of 1736, his eldest son, Jean-Baptiste, and twenty other men were killed near Fort Saint-Charles by the Sioux. Despite this grim reminder of the dangers of taking sides in native wars, La Vérendrye pressed on. In 1738 he established Fort La Reine on the Assiniboine River (on the site of present-day Portage la Prairie). Later that year he explored southwest to the Missouri River, an area inhabited by the Mandan people. He made friends with the Mandan, but exhausted and disappointed that the Missouri River flowed to the south and not toward the Pacific, he returned to Montreal in January 1739. In his place, his sons hoped to find a route to the northwest up the Saskatchewan River.

Below **A traditional birch-bark canoe, light yet resilient.**

Above **Fort William on Lake Superior, pictured here in 1857, was from 1805 the wilderness headquarters of the North West Company, a major force in the Canadian fur trade.**

THE VÉRENDRYE SONS

La Vérendrye's sons had been leading expeditions of their own since the establishment of the first post on Rainy Lake in 1731. In 1742 Louis and François left Fort La Reine with orders to travel as far to the west as possible. After reaching the Great Plains of present-day South Dakota, they put their faith, as their father had done, in the goodwill of native peoples, who guided them to the Cheyenne River. Some historians believe they traveled as far as the Big Horn Mountains in western Wyoming. Meanwhile, Pierre returned to the west and built Fort Dauphin on Lake Dauphin and Fort Bourbon at the mouth of the Saskatchewan on Cedar Lake.

END OF THE DREAM

In 1744 La Vérendrye returned to Montreal exhausted and heavily in debt. He planned another expedition to the west, but the government had lost faith in him and refused to support his ventures. His sons Louis and Pierre continued to build new forts and explored as far as the forks of the Saskatchewan River. La Vérendrye died in 1749, the same year in which the new French naval minister awarded him a captaincy and a medal.

La Vérendrye's son Louis-Joseph wrote about the hard-won recognition of his family's contribution to exploration of Canada:

Here more than elsewhere, envy remains a passion much in fashion, from which it is not possible to protect oneself. . . . Even as my father with my brothers and myself was wearing himself out with fatigue and expenditure, his efforts were represented as directed only toward the discovery of beaver, his forced expenditures as nothing but dissipation [wasteful spending], his communications as nothing but lies. Envy in this country does not exist in half-measures.

Louis-Joseph de La Vérendrye, in a letter of September 30, 1750

SEE ALSO
- France • Lewis and Clark Expedition
- Native Peoples

GLOSSARY

anchorage A place suitable for anchoring a ship.

anthropology The study of human beings, especially in relation to their society and culture.

astrolabe An instrument used to determine the position of the sun, moon, stars, and planets.

caravel A small, fast Spanish or Portuguese ship with lateen (triangular) sails.

Crusade One of several Christian military expeditions, especially in the eleventh, twelfth, and thirteenth centuries, whose purpose was to regain the Holy Land from the Muslims.

dhow A light yet strong wooden ship, with triangular sails and a short mast, used by medieval Arab traders.

equinox A twice-yearly event, usually occurring around March 22 and September 22, when the sun crosses the celestial equator and day and night are of equal length.

Franciscan A member of one of the Roman Catholic religious orders of men or women founded by Saint Francis of Assisi in 1209 or an offshoot of one of those orders.

frieze An ornamental sculptured band on a building or piece of furniture.

geology The study of the origin and structure of the earth.

intendant A senior official in New France who was in charge of economic affairs and represented the governor in his absence.

Jesuit A member of a Roman Catholic religious order known for its educational and missionary work.

latitude Measurement of a point on the earth's surface north or south of the equator.

league A unit of distance equal to three miles.

longitude Measurement of a point on the earth's surface east or west of a given prime meridian.

magnetic storm A major disturbance in the earth's magnetic field.

malaria A fever caused by a parasite transmitted by the bite of the female anopheles mosquito.

meridian An imaginary line, running from the North to the South Pole, used to indicate longitude.

monopoly Total control over the sale of a good or service in a given area.

monsoon A wind in southern Asia that blows from the northeast in winter and from the southwest in summer, when it is accompanied by heavy rains.

mutiny A revolt against authority, especially of a ship's crew against its officers.

parallel An imaginary line, circling the globe parallel to the equator, used to indicate latitude.

planisphere A representation of all or part of the spherical earth on a flat surface.

portage The carrying of boats overland from one waterway to another.

prime meridian An imaginary line that runs from the North to the South Pole through Greenwich, England, and marks zero degrees longitude.

reconnaissance A preliminary survey to gain information.

scurvy A serious disease caused by lack of vitamin C; its symptoms include bleeding and sponginess in the gums.

sextant An instrument used by seafarers and explorers to measure the height of the sun or a star above the horizon and thus give an estimation of one's latitude.

Sherpa A member of a Tibetan people living in the Himalayas who provide support for mountain climbers.

Sioux A member of a Native American people who lived on the Great Plains and the western fringes of the Great Lakes.

sultan Title of a secular Muslim ruler, especially of the Ottoman Empire.

viceroy Ruler representing the authority of a king or queen in a colonial territory.

INDEX